COLLINS GEM

THE
SEASHORE

Text by Rosalind Fitter
Illustrations by Susan...

HarperCollins*Publ...*

HarperCollins Publishers
PO Box, Glasgow G4 0NB

First published 1984

Reprint 10 9 8

© Rosalind Fitter (text) 1984
  Susanna Ray (illustrations) 1984

ISBN 0 00 458824 X
All rights reserved

Printed in Italy by Amadeus S.p.A., Rome

Contents

Note on abbreviations used in the text
In order to provide as much information as possible
in this Gem Guide, abbreviations have been adopted
for the generally accepted zones of the shore, e.g.
MHWS. These are explained in the diagram on page 7.
Male ♂ and female ♀ symbols are also used.

Introduction

The area uncovered by the tide—the boundary between sea and land—is a fascinating, ever-changing environment. The seashore has a very rich flora and fauna because of its great variety of habitats, some sunlit, others more shaded, both in or on rock, on or under weed, in pools, under stones, in crevices, in sand or mud, and so on. The sea constantly replenishes the supply of oxygen, nutrients and food, and the salt content of sea-water (around 3.5‰) is constant, while its temperature varies only gradually between an average 16°C in September to 6°C in February. To its inhabitants, it is a very equable environment, though waves and tides pose special problems.

There are two high and two low tides in approximately 24 hours round all the British coast, except in the Solent which has double that number. The times and level of high and low water are predictable because they depend on the movements of the earth and the moon, and they can be found from tide tables. They vary in a lunar month from **spring** tide, when water reaches highest and lowest on the shore, at full and new moon, to **neap** tides when there is least rise and fall. Spring tides occur fortnightly, but the greatest are in March and September; collecting down at low water at these times can be very exciting as organisms not normally uncovered such as blue-rayed limpet, sea urchins, sea-squirts and the plumose anemone are exposed. These daily tidal movements are caused by the gravitational pull of the moon; springs occur when the sun lines up with the moon and augments its pull, neaps when they are at right angles. The fortnightly rhythm arises from the lunar month of 28 days, the time it takes for the moon to circle the earth.

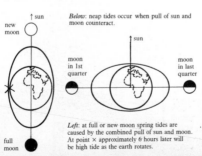

↑ sun

new moon

full moon

Below: neap tides occur when pull of sun and moon counteract.

↑ sun

moon in 1st quarter

moon in last quarter

Left: at full or new moon spring tides are caused by the combined pull of sun and moon. At point × approximately 6 hours later will be high tide as the earth rotates.

Different communities of plants and animals occur at different vertical levels because some are better able to withstand drying out when the tide recedes. This **zonation** is especially well marked on rocky shores where bands of lichens of different hue on the rocks in the splash zone lie above a series of wracks, each of which thrives at a particular level. Unlike seaweeds, lichens are not algae, but a closely interdependent symbiotic association of an alga with a fungus. Very slow growing, they can withstand the extremes of drought and temperature characteristic of the splash zone, which is never or rarely submerged.

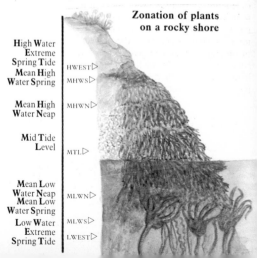

Zonation of plants on a rocky shore

High Water Extreme Spring Tide — HWEST ▷

Mean High Water Spring — MHWS ▷

Mean High Water Neap — MHWN ▷

Mid Tide Level — MTL ▷

Mean Low Water Neap — MLWN ▷

Mean Low Water Spring — MLWS ▷

Low Water Extreme Spring Tide — LWEST ▷

So well defined are the bands that you can tell how high you are on the shore by the species of wrack present, and the sight of the bent stipes (stalks) of kelp indicates low tide. Many other groups of related species are zoned, each species kept within its level by its superior ability to survive in those particular conditions. Thus, in general the periwinkles—small, rough, edible and flat—occur in series down the shore; as do the toothed, purple and grey topshells. The acorn barnacle is found below the star barnacle where they occur together, but extends into its zone in the colder northern waters where the star barnacle cannot survive. Both species occur above two other barnacles, *Balanus perforatus* and *B. crenatus*.

Shore communities also vary with the strength of wind and wave. Really exposed rocky shores have very few seaweeds—they get torn off by waves, and only occur in pools. Instead barnacles or com-

Costa protetta

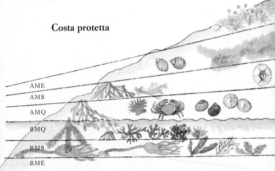

AME
AMS
AMQ
BMQ
BMS
BME

mon mussels, both of which are firmly attached, often form a complete cover, along with dog whelks which eat them, common limpets and beadlet anemones. Tiny rough periwinkles hide in empty barnacle shells and small periwinkles, which browse lichens, occur high up in splash zone crevices. Both these snails are well adapted to this semi-terrestrial habitat, and unlike other seashore snails, the rough periwinkle does not rely on the sea for reproduction—it produces miniature shelled young.

Where there is more shelter, algal sporelings can become attached, and once established the weed movement prevents barnacle settlement. The weeds are food for many browsers, mainly sea-slugs, snails and some sea urchins, as well as damp shelter for other animals. The characteristic communities at different shore levels on exposed and more sheltered shores are shown below.

Very exposed shore

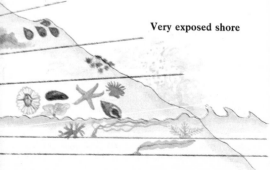

Plants are essential to nearly all natural communities, for they are the organisms which actually trap the energy of the sun into the food on which all animals depend. At sea, only tiny floating algae (phytoplankton) can get sufficient light for photosynthesis, but the shore allows seaweeds to attach and receive plentiful light. The bladders possessed by many seaweeds help buoyancy when covered, lifting the fronds towards the light. The 'forests' of kelp and wracks look quite different when covered, and cut out over 90% of the light. The holdfasts harbour a wealth of small animals such as the banded chink shell, scaleworms, ribbon worms, brittle stars, polychaetes and epiphytic plants. Kelps were once collected for agar, and wracks for manure.

Drying out is the main problem for seaweeds, for they lack the cuticle of higher plants, but a thick mucous layer compensates to some extent. Channelled wrack can tolerate several days in a dry black, brittle state. The most beautiful, delicate and numerous seaweeds are the reds, found low on more sheltered shores. They are best identified under water and you can preserve fine greens and reds by floating them on to paper before drying. This is particularly successful with feathery reds. It is often difficult to distinguish the pigments in algae; some browns look green and reds brown, especially when old, and all bleach white.

For animals, desiccation and temperature variation are also problems, overcome in various ways; while the tide is out, many hide in cracks (the sea slater or rough periwinkle), others close opercula (barnacles and most snails) or tentacles (anemones), clamp down like limpets, or rest under damp weed (ribbonworms, ragworms, crabs) or boulders (chitons, brittlestars, crabs).

Pools on the lower shore, especially if deep and with plenty of oxygen-producing weeds, offer a more constant habitat and harbour many species more characteristic of zones further down the shore, such as the seaweeds sea belt, thongweed, *Cystoseira*, *Codium* and peacock's tail, as well as prawns and spider crabs. Shallow upper-shore pools can, however, suffer wide fluctuations of acidity, temperature and salinity, which makes them more hostile environments.

Most shore animals have microscopic plank-tonic larvae which ensure dispersal. How the larvae eventually settle on an appropriate shore at the right level is still not fully under-stood, though it is known that in barnacles chemicals from adults are detected in the sea-water. A look through a simple microscope at seawater can reveal the beautiful plants and animals of the plankton—an important food source for shore animals.

Whether rock, shingle, sand or mud forms the shoreline depends on the softness of the rock, the force and direction of the waves, and the presence of deposits brought down by rivers. Shingle accumulates on storm beaches, where waves are too strong to allow small grains to settle; large stones roll freely and no water is held between the stones. Nothing much lives here except a few deep-rooted plants above the high-tide level.

Where particle size is smaller, water is held between the grains by capillary action even at low tide, and the presence of organic matter helps colonisation. The top few centimetres of sandy shores are moved by the waves, pre-venting the establishment of large plants; with no cover from predators or desiccation the best mode of life for animals is burrowing. When exposed by the tide, sandy and muddy shors appear almost lifeless but tracks, holes and depressions, casts and spouts of water all

12

betray the presence of many animals in the fairly constant environment a few centimetres below the surface.

In fairly clean sand the banded wedge shell is very common, even in quite exposed sands, along with the thin tellin, sunset and trough shells, razors, cockles (20 cm down), lugworm, sand mason and other fan worms, the polychaete *Nerine* and amphipod *Corophium*; all of these are deposit or suspension feeders, which lie still and draw in debris directly or else filter it from a water current created by beating hairs. Weever fish, sand eels, shrimps, common goby, sandhoppers, the isopod *Eurydice*, polychaetes such as *Glycera* and *Neanthes diversicolor*, the necklace shell and, low on the shore, even burrowing starfish, brittle stars and the masked crab are scavengers or carnivores. A shrimp net trawled along the water's edge often yields a rewarding catch, as does casting a torch beam on a damp sand surface at night. The base of the food chains here are a few small algae, and bacteria and fungi feeding on debris brought in by the tide; all live in the water between the grains.

Some beaches provide a rich variety of bivalve shells, washed up from deeper water. Some are very beautiful; many will have a hole bored near the hinge by the predatory necklace shell. At high tide oxygen is renewed, and crabs, flatfish and common gobies which

13

have come inshore, as well as crustaceans, molluscs and worms, search the surface for food: at low tide wading birds feast.

A sheltered and muddier shore like a harbour supports a huge number of animals as the organic content is greater and habitat less shifting, and species such as the otter shell, rayed artemis, carpet shell, tube worms (*Amphitrite* and *Cirriformia*), carnivorous nemertine and polychaete worms such as *Phyllodoce* and *Perinereis* are added to the fauna.

Deoxygenation and silt clogging the filtering apparatus are, however, problems: the numerous bacteria use much oxygen in muds. The black, smelly anaerobic layer is not far below the surface and water spaces which hold oxygen are smaller between fine grains. The aeration of burrows is very important and fan worms, lugworms, *Corophium*, and others create water currents which achieve this, while suspension and deposit-feeding bivalves remove oxygen as well as food from the material they draw in.

The soft mud flats of estuaries have a fluctuating salinity, often reduced to below 1‰ at low water, which fewer species can tolerate, but those present

Examples of burrowing depths

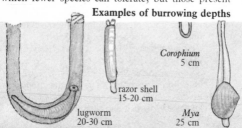

Corophium
5 cm

razor shell
15-20 cm

lugworm
20-30 cm

Mya
25 cm

are in vast numbers. The amphipod *Gammarus zaddachi*, the isopod *Sphaeroma*, some mysids and the tiny laver spire snail, thrive in brackish water as do the flounder and common goby. Cord-grass and eel-grass are typical of mud flats, and on any stones, horned wrack and *Enteromorpha* may be found, along with edible and rough periwinkles, shore crabs and mussels; indeed estuaries often support enough mussels and cockles for commercial gathering. Besides some polychaetes, such as lugworms, cat worms and *Neanthes diversicolor*, the amphipod *Corophium*, the Baltic tellin and peppery furrow shell occur in sufficient density easily to sustain flocks of waders; in a day's feeding a small wader can consume several hundred Baltic tellins or many thousand *Corophium*.

The key which follows will direct you to the group to which your species belongs, and to the relevant plates and descriptions. The book contains the commonest plants and animals, as well as a few rarer but well known species.

Treat the shore with respect—replace boulders and stones and return animals to their correct part of the shore. Left in unaerated water, animals quickly die.

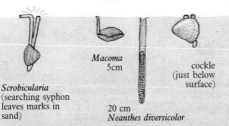

Scrobicularia
(searching syphon
leaves marks in
sand)

Macoma
5cm

20 cm
Neanthes diversicolor

cockle
(just below
surface)

Guide to seashore plants and animals

Plants

Algae
green 22-25
brown 27-37
red 38-51
Covered by every tide. Browns may fade to green and reds look brownish

Lichens
Ramalina, Lichina 50-51
Above high water mark

Flowering plants 52-69

Plant-like (but lacking plant pigments)

Sea firs 74-75
Transparent and rigid. Polyps have tentacles

Soft coral 80-81
Flesh-coloured lobes with white polyps

Feather star 172-3
10 feathery reddish arms

Hornwrack 170-1
Buff with network of tiny 'cells'

Encrusting

Some algae and lichens 50-51
*Pink in pools; black or orange
above high water mark*

Sponges 72-73
Soft, brightly coloured with pores

Seamats 170-1
*Round base of weeds. Many tiny
'cells' visible*

Compound sea-squirts 186-7
*Brightly coloured colonies,
often star-shaped*

Tentacles

Jellyfish 76-77
Swimming with tentacles hanging down

Sea anemones 78-81
*Attached with tentacles and mouth
upwards*

Sea gooseberry 76-77
*Swimming, transparent, 2 trailing
tentacles*

Cuttlefish, squid, octopus 138-9
10 or 8 suckered tentacles

Worm-like or slug-like

Flatworms 82-83
Small, flat, leaf-like

Ribbon worms 84-85
Soft, no bristles, have proboscis; often coiled round weed

Segmented worms with lateral bristles:
Scale worms 88-89
Scales or hair on back

Rag, rock, cat & paddle worms 90-93
Active worms with tentacles on head & large lateral lobes or paddles
Burrowing worms 100-1
In sand or mud

Burrowing bivalve
Teredo 124-5
2 small shells at end of worm-like body

Sea cucumbers 182-3
Usually 5 rows of tubefeet. Branched tentacles round mouth

Sea slugs 120-3
Foot, tentacles on head; usually feathery gills on back

Tubes

Made by sedentary segmented worms 94-99
Calcareous, or of mud or sand

Burrowed in rock
    Polydora 98-99
    Bivalves 124-5
    In bivalve shells
    Sponge *Cliona* 72-73
    Limnoria 148-9
    In wood

Shell

Barnacles
    firmly attached to rock 142-3
    with stalk 144-5

Chitons 104-5
8 overlapping plates; mollusc foot beneath

Snails 106-119
Single shell, foot

Bivalves 126-137
2 shells, foot within

Sea urchins 178-9
Spherical or flattened shell, 5-radial symmetry, spines

Distinct legs

Hard outer covering: ARTHROPODS

More than 5 pairs walking or swimming legs:
  Mysids 146-7
  Shrimp-like, no pincers
  Isopods 148-151
  Slaters, lacking carapace
  Amphipods 152-3
  Lateral flattening, no carapace

5 pairs of walking legs, 1st pair with pincers
  Decapods 154-165
  Shrimps, prawns, lobsters, crabs

4 pairs of legs
  Pycnogonids 166-7

3 pairs of legs
  Insects 166-7

Internal backbone: VERTEBRATES

Birds 204-225

Seals, otter 226-7

Sac-like body

Sponges *Grantia, Sycon* 72-73

Comb jelly *Beroë* 76-77

Sea cucumber 182-3
Branched contractile tentacles round mouth, usually 5 rows of tube feet

Sea squirts 184-5
2 siphons, squirt water

Parasitic barnacles 144-5
On abdomen of crabs

Distinct arms usually 5; tube feet beneath

Starfish 172-5
Stout arms, no well defined central disc

Brittlestars 176-7
Central disc; long, fine, fragile arms

Active swimmers

Fish 188-201

Marine mammals 226-9
No scales, warm-blooded

Cuttlefish, squid 138-9
10 suckered tentacles

21

Green seaweeds

Seaweeds are algae, the most primitive plants. Although all higher plants are green, because of the photosynthetic pigment chlorophyll, many seaweeds have other photosynthetic pigments as well, so that they may seem brown, red or (in some planktonic types not covered here) yellowish. Colour is a fundamental distinction in algae.

The middle reaches of rocky coasts, especially where there is freshwater seepage or even sewage outfall, are often coated by bright green **sea lettuce** *Ulva lactuca* **1**, which has broad, irregularly shaped, translucent fronds, usually 10-20 cm long, and attached by a short stalk. *Enteromorpha intestinalis* **2** has pale green, inflated tubular fronds, 1.5 cm in diameter and up to 60 cm long, attached by a disc to rocks in pools on the upper shore. The air within, which aids buoyancy and keeps the fronds near the well-lit surface of the water, and the irregular constrictions make it resemble guts, hence the name. *E. compressa* **3** differs in being branched, and the branches may be compressed. Both favour brackish water and are most abundant in spring, turning white in late summer. *Prasiola stipitata* **4** is a small, stalked, dark green plant to 2.5 cm, found high on rocky coasts. All these green seaweeds occur on all coasts.

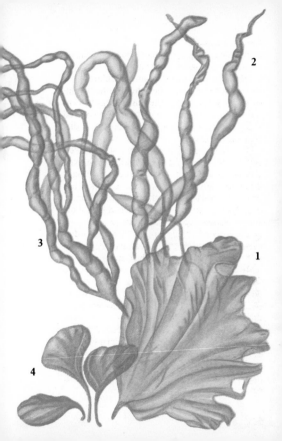

Green seaweeds

Codium tomentosum **1** has sturdy, cylindrical, spongy, dark green fronds, 25-35 cm long, with a velvety look. This and its sister species *C. fragile* are the only British members of an otherwise tropical group of seaweeds. Found in deep mid- and lower littoral pools in the south and west and much eaten by sea-slugs.

The other species here are formed of finer threads. *Cladophora rupestris* **2** is a common, dark dull green, much branched plant,

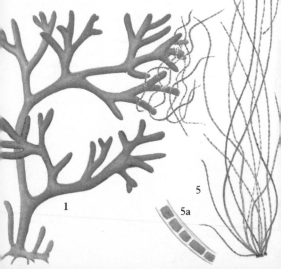

1

5

5a

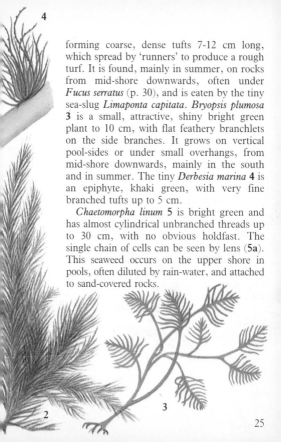

forming coarse, dense tufts 7-12 cm long, which spread by 'runners' to produce a rough turf. It is found, mainly in summer, on rocks from mid-shore downwards, often under *Fucus serratus* (p. 30), and is eaten by the tiny sea-slug *Limaponta capitata*. *Bryopsis plumosa* **3** is a small, attractive, shiny bright green plant to 10 cm, with flat feathery branchlets on the side branches. It grows on vertical pool-sides or under small overhangs, from mid-shore downwards, mainly in the south and in summer. The tiny *Derbesia marina* **4** is an epiphyte, khaki green, with very fine branched tufts up to 5 cm.

Chaetomorpha linum **5** is bright green and has almost cylindrical unbranched threads up to 30 cm, with no obvious holdfast. The single chain of cells can be seen by lens (**5a**). This seaweed occurs on the upper shore in pools, often diluted by rain-water, and attached to sand-covered rocks.

Brown seaweeds: kelps

Kelps are the dominant weeds of the lower shore. The first two are only fully exposed at extreme low water, but at most other low tides the stipes (stalks) stand out of the water with fronds drooping back.

Oarweed or **tangle** *Laminaria digitata* **1** has a spreading holdfast and a thick smooth flexible stipe, oval in cross-section. As with **cuvie** *L. hyperborea* **2** the young plants have entire fronds which, as they age, split into shiny leathery straps, especially on rough coasts. *L. hyperborea* is found below *L. digitata* on exposed shores and in deep pools. Its hard, rough, tapering stipe, arising from a root-like, down-growing, more confined holdfast, affords good anchorage to epiphytes, including *Lomentaria articulata* (p. 44) and *Rhodymenia* (*Palmaria*) *palmata* **2a** (p. 38). It dies back in autumn and regrows from the base each spring. The stipes yield agar.

Sea belt or **sugar kelp** *L. saccharina* **3** is a long, narrow, crinkled, yellow-brown belt, 10-15 cm by 1.5 m or more. It grows in deep pools or attached to small stones or rocks on sandflats near low water on more sheltered shores, where it drapes rocks. It exudes a sweet white sugary substance when dry, and can be used as a weatherstrap.

26

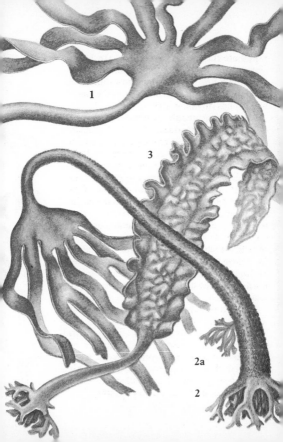

1

3

2a

2

Brown seaweeds
Furbelows *Saccorhiza polyschides* **1** grows singly at MLWS and below. Its flattened, twisted, frilly-edged stipe opens out into a massive fan-like frond, like **oarweed** (p. 26) but larger, up to 4.5 m. Though the largest British seaweed, it is a summer annual, commonest in the south and west. **Dabberlocks** *Alaria esculenta* **2** is distinguished from it and from the kelps by its more delicate, olive-yellow, leaf-like frond, with well-defined midrib and yellowish fruiting bodies ('keys') at the base of the stipe. It is only found near low water and below on very exposed shores, where it replaces **oarweed**, and is commonest in winter and in the north. In sheltered situations, just below low water, the long unbranched fronds of another annual, **sea bootlace** *Chorda filum* **3** form tangled masses in summer. The hollow, slender, cylindrical thongs can extend 6-7 m from a tiny holdfast. The cords are slimy, hairy when young, and as adults often carry epiphytes such as *Litosiphon* (p. 36). The superficially similar **thongweed** *Himanthalia elongata* **4** grows from a small button (4a) in winter into flattened, branched, yellow-brown straps, up to 2.5 m and often blotched with fruiting bodies; found in deep pools on exposed shores around low water.

4a

4

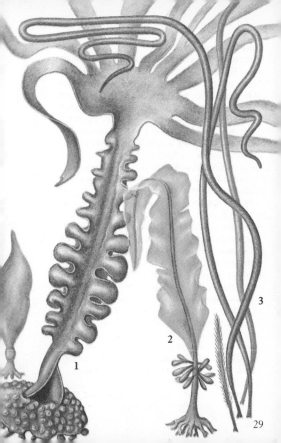

1

2

3

29

Brown seaweeds: wracks

Very prominent above the kelps on rocky shores are the wracks *Fucus*, which show clear zonation. All are tough, olive-brown weeds with a short stipe, which continues as a mid-rib. Their branches fork regularly and swollen sexual structures (receptacles) form at the tips.

Except on exposed shores, the upper middle zone supports **spiral wrack** *F. spiralis* **1** which is very resistant to desiccation. Its smooth-edged fronds, 12 mm wide and 15-30 cm long, are twisted near the tips, which develop oval orange receptacles, translucent at the rim. **Bladder wrack** *F. vesiculosus* **2** is abundant and variable, and occupies the mid-shore band on shores of slight to moderate exposure. Its fronds may be over 1 m long and have wavy edges and typically paired air-bladders. On exposed coasts it has fewer bladders. The side branches of female plants have swollen yellow receptacles, the male orange.

Saw or **toothed wrack** *F. serratus* **3** grows below bladder wrack, on the lower mid-shore. The bushy plants, to 60 cm, have serrated edges, no bladders, flat receptacles, and are often covered with epizoites **3a** such as *Spirorbis* (p. 94). **Horned wrack** *F. ceranoides* **4** is a brackish-water species often attached to stones in estuaries. It is smaller, more delicate, and has pointed receptacles in fan-like clusters.

3a

Brown seaweeds

The seaweed found highest on rocky shores is **channelled wrack** *Pelvetia canaliculata* **1**. After long exposure, it appears as small black brittle tufts, 5-15 cm. When wetted it is olive-brown, with incurled margins, but no midrib or air bladders. **Egg** or **knotted wrack** *Ascophyllum nodosum* **2**, is common on midshore and often replaces bladder wrack (p. 30) on sheltered shores, reaching 3 m. The narrow fronds are olive-green with no midrib, irregularly branching, with single egg-shaped, unpoppable bladders; it has yellowish stalked receptacles in spring and summer. The fronds often carry tufts of *Polysiphonia lanosa* **2a** (p. 42). **Sea oak** *Halidrys siliquosa* **3** is a widespread perennial, 30-120 cm, found in deep pools or below low water mark on sheltered shores. It has a small, strong conical holdfast and alternate spiky branches. The narrow, pointed, banded air-bladders have short stalks; the similar receptacles occur at the branch tips. *Bifurcaria bifurcata* **4**, found attached to sides of deep pools in the south-west, differs in its creeping holdfast and long, blunt fruiting bodies. The round stipe is yellowish-green and fronds may have single air-bladders. *Dictyota dichotoma* **5** is small (to 15 cm), flat and pale olive, and found in shallow pools and on rocks below low water mark, mainly in the south-west. The delicate, equally-forking fronds, 4-5 cm wide, have no midrib.

2a

Brown seaweeds

Peacock's tail *Padina pavonia* **1** is a beautiful pale brown weed found in summer to late autumn on the edges of sunny mid- and lower shore pools in the south-west. The mature fronds form erect funnel-shaped whorls, 5-12 cm, banded outside and lime-encrusted inside, and fringed with fine hairs on top. The similarly distributed *Cystoseira tamariscifolia* **2** has intricate, bushy fronds, appearing iridescent blue-green when submerged. It is profusely-branched, 30-45 cm, with many spines or 'leaves', 3 mm long, and small bladders beneath the tufted oval receptacles at the branch tips (**2a**). The hollow, unbranched fronds of *Asperococcus fistulosus* **3** are common in summer on weed or rocks in mid-shore pools. The tufts, green when young but olive and stippled with tiny bristles when mature, arise from a disc holdfast and widen to 'tubes' 15-30 cm long and about 1 cm wide, slightly constricted at intervals. The similar *Scytosiphon lomentaria* **4** has slimy unbranched hollow fronds, constricted every 2 cm, like a string of tiny sausages; com monest in winter, often on exposed shores. The thin, oval, pointed, leaf-like fronds of *Punctaria plantaginea* 5 are olive-brown, soft and slimy to the touch, and dark-spotted, with a bristly stipe. Common in the warmer months in mid-shore pools on stones, shells and rocks, it dies back in autumn. *Petalonia fascia*, though similar, is smaller, has no spots and is commonest in winter.

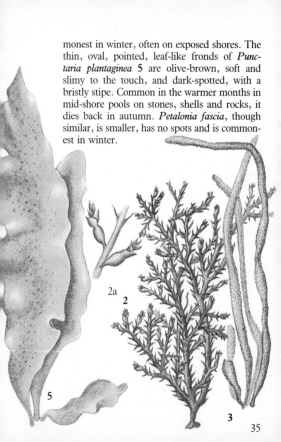

2a
2

5

3

Brown seaweeds

Although *Desmarestia* species are really sublittoral, they are often cast ashore in spring and summer, entangled with kelp stipes. *D. aculeata* 1, a perennial, is about 1 m long, with alternate branches bearing rings of tufts in summer. *D. lingulata*, an annual of the south and west, has a flattened leafy frond with primary and secondary branches, narrowest at their bases. Both decompose rapidly out of water.

The other seaweeds on this page are epiphytes—that is, they grow on other seaweeds. *Leathesia difformis* 2 is a small, shiny olive-brown plant which forms a thick, wavy-walled bulbous mass, up to 2.5 cm across, round the stipes of other weeds and on rocks. Solid when young, it becomes hollow later. It is abundant in summer. *Ectocarpus confervoides* 3 is very abundant and consists of yellow-green branching filaments, 12-30 cm, and so fine (often only one cell thick) and intricate that it looks cloudy in water, but hangs matted and limp when in air. *E. tomentosus* has 'ropey' fronds.

Sphacelaria cirrhosa 4 is common all year on the lower shore, often on *Fucus*. Its tufts of stiff threads, up to 2.5 cm long with regular opposite branchlets, look feathery under a lens. Filaments grow out from the disc holdfast as runners and give rise to new plants. *Litosiphon pusillus* 5, in contrast, has unbranched tufts, soft, slimy and yellowish, and up to 10 cm long. It grows only on *Chorda filum* and is abundant in summer.

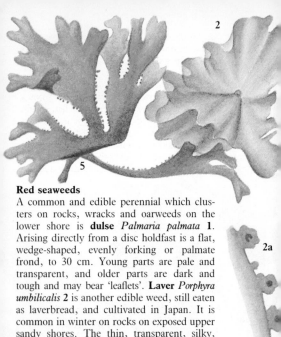

Red seaweeds

A common and edible perennial which clusters on rocks, wracks and oarweeds on the lower shore is **dulse** *Palmaria palmata* **1**. Arising directly from a disc holdfast is a flat, wedge-shaped, evenly forking or palmate frond, to 30 cm. Young parts are pale and transparent, and older parts are dark and tough and may bear 'leaflets'. **Laver** *Porphyra umbilicalis* **2** is another edible weed, still eaten as laverbread, and cultivated in Japan. It is common in winter on rocks on exposed upper sandy shores. The thin, transparent, silky, almost circular frond, up to 20 cm across, is brownish-red but quickly fades greenish, then resembling *Ulva* (p. 22). Exposed by the tide, it clings like black plastic to rocks.

The flat, rounded, gelatinous and opaque, blood-red fronds of **red rags** *Dilsea carnosa* **3** are attached to rocks in sandy places from midshore down. Several short rounded stipes grow from a disc holdfast, and the old fronds become tough and ragged. It is more abundant in the south, as is *Calliblepharis ciliata* **4**, 10-20 cm, whose short stipe arises from a root-like holdfast and widens into flat, tough, dull dark red fronds, with side branches. This and *Callophyllis laciniata* **5**, a smaller, bright crimson, palmate plant, to 8 cm, with wrinkled margins, are really sub-littoral; common on *Laminaria hyperborea* and in driftweed.

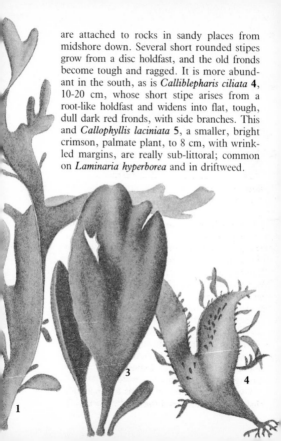

Epiphytic red seaweeds

All these seaweeds are generally found as epiphytes low on the shore on laminarian stipes or in deep shady pools. **Sea oak** *Phycodrys rubens* **1** has deeply indented, leaf-like, browny-crimson fronds with midrib and veins, resembling an oak or holly leaf. In winter only the midrib persists. New leaves grow in spring, with spores on branchlets arising from the veins. *Delesseria sanguinea* **2** is similar but larger (to 40 cm), less branched, with darker pink, leaf-like fronds with no indentations, and opposite veins. In spring spore-producing outgrowths and new leaflets arise from the old midribs. Both are common, especially in summer, and make beautiful dried specimens. *Membranoptera alata* **3** is very common; its deep crimson, ribbon-like fronds, 7-12 cm, have much irregular, alternate branching in one plane. The frond ends are pointed, often notched, and faint paired veins arise from the prominent midrib. *Hypoglossum woodwardii* **4**, common in the south, grows as a bushy, rose-pink plant, to 15 cm, often with several stipes from one disc holdfast, which has root-like projections round the edge. The stipe continues as a midrib along the length of the frond, but there are no lateral veins, unlike **3** and **5**. Pointed branches arise alternately at right angles. The rarer *Apoglossum ruscifolium* **5** is darker rose-red, with broader, wavy, fronds, with rounded tips and faint parallel veins.

Red seaweeds

The parasite *Polysiphonia lanosa* **1** grows on the scars of the fruiting bodies of *Ascophyllum nodosum*, or occasionally *Fucus* spp. The dense tufts of branched, hair-like threads (to 5 cm) are very common, and can reduce buoyancy so much that the host is torn away in heavy seas. The other weeds here have a delicate feathery structure, best seen in water. *Ptilota plumosa* **2** is a northern species common on laminarian stipes. The smooth, firm main stem (to 30 cm)

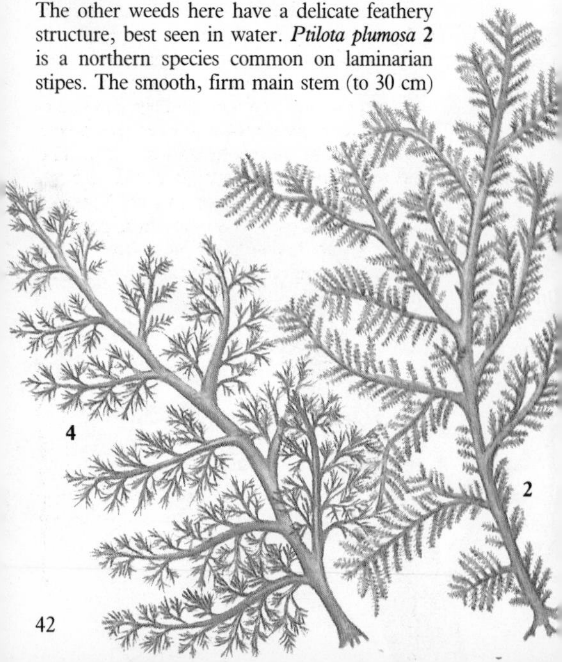

4

2

has irregular flattened side-branches, which themselves bear feathery opposite branchlets, tapering at both ends. *Plumaria elegans* **3** is similar, but has a ragged stem, is smaller and less common, though found also in the south. Its soft fronds, translucent at the tips and often bearing common purse sponge, favour shaded gulleys or hang limply from overhangs. *Heterosiphonia plumosa* **4**, 15-20 cm, is deep rich crimson, with a hairy, tapering main axis from which alternate, flattened, feathery branches arise, bare at the base, but dividing into spear-shaped branchlets; on rocks or weeds at extreme low water, but more often washed up. The limp soft fronds of *Lomentaria clavellosa* **5**, to 30 cm, are found in summer only on the under surface of overhangs, or in low shore pools on weeds. Several hollow stems arise from a disc holdfast, bearing alternate feathery branches which are elliptical in outline.

Red seaweeds

The glistening pale crimson fronds of *Lomentaria articulata* **1** are formed of chains of oval beads, branching at constrictions. It is iridescent in water and common on exposed rock faces. **Cockscomb** *Plocamium cartilagineum* **2**,  though sublittoral, is frequently washed up and the rose-red fronds are beautiful when mounted; they bear groups of 3 or 4 compound side-branches, all on one side, above an awl-like bare branch; such groups alternate up the stem, and branchlets occur on the upper side of each branch only (fruiting body **2a** also shown). A very common small plant found on overhangs or edging pools is *Gelidium corneum* **3**. It is a very dark translucent garnet red, 2-10 cm, with a rigid, horny texture. It spreads by creeping rhizomes. The branches are variously arranged, but always taper at the base and are pointed at the tip. **Pepper dulse** *Laurencia pinnatifida* **4** with its strong acrid smell, is abundant on most shores, especially in winter. It is very variable, to 30 cm, but much shorter on rocks high on shore, and red, olive or even yellowy on sunny sites. It forms firm dense tufts, branching repeatedly and alternately in one plane, the rounded tips shaped like playing-card clubs. *Odonthalia dentata* **5** is another tufted species, northern and often cast ashore. The opaque flattened fronds, 7-15 cm, with serrated tips, are dark purplish, but easily bleached.

44

Red seaweeds

The firm, round, brownish-purple stems of *Gastroclonium ovatum* **1**, 5-15 cm, come from a disc holdfast, and its bushy branches bear clusters of paler, oval, spore-producing bladders; commonest in the south on the lower shore. The entangled, rigid tufts of *Ahnfeltia plicata* **2**, 7-15 cm, are found on rocks low on exposed shores, and grow from a greyish crust-like holdfast. This plant, dark purple but black when dry, resembles tangled wire, hence its French name 'fil de fer'. The bright crimson *Griffithsia flosculosa* **3**, 7-20 cm, grows in similar habitats, but its branched threads are more pliable, though erect in water. Small dots all over the filaments are reproductive spheres.

Dumontia incrassata **4** grows up to 50 cm from a small holdfast and branches alternately and irregularly from near the base. The cylindrical fronds become hollow with age. This and *Cystoclonium purpureum* **5** are common summer annuals throughout Britain, mostly in midshore pools where sunlight may bleach them to olive.

C. purpureum has soft thin branches, tapering at both ends to pointed tips, and with dark red swellings (reproductive bodies) in summer. The perennial *Gracilaria verrucosa* **6**, 5-30 cm, grows from a small disc. It is less bushy, has longer branches, and is common on midshore rocks, often partially sand-covered.

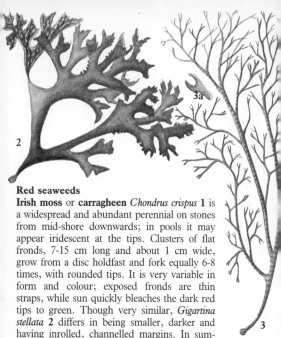

Red seaweeds

Irish moss or **carragheen** *Chondrus crispus* **1** is a widespread and abundant perennial on stones from mid-shore downwards; in pools it may appear iridescent at the tips. Clusters of flat fronds, 7-15 cm long and about 1 cm wide, grow from a disc holdfast and fork equally 6-8 times, with rounded tips. It is very variable in form and colour; exposed fronds are thin straps, while sun quickly bleaches the dark red tips to green. Though very similar, *Gigartina stellata* **2** differs in being smaller, darker and having inrolled, channelled margins. In summer and autumn spore-producing bodies like grape pips appear all over the frond tips. Dense colonies occur on most shores, even if very exposed. Old specimens are often encrusted with the bryozoan *Flustrellidra hispida* (p. 170). The bushy, rather stiff tufts of *Ceramium rub* *rum* **3**, to 30 cm, are a very common sight on stones, weeds and in pools on mid-shore. The fine branched threads vary from garnet-red to greenish, but have pincer-like tips and dark bands (**3a**). Though similar in length, the twiggy, glossy, rounded frond of *Furcellaria lumbricalis* **4** arises from a branching holdfast (thus differing from the disc of the otherwise similar *Polyides*) and divides by regular, equal forking 6-8 times. In summer the tips bear long pointed pods; in pools low on the shore.

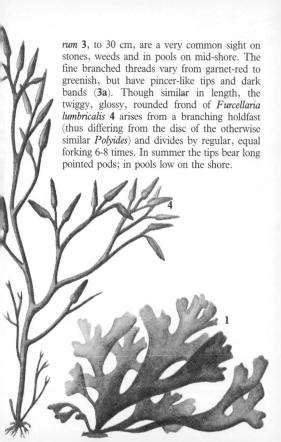

Encrusting red seaweeds and lichens
Coralweed *Corallina officinalis* **1** is a pinkish coral-like plant, 2-12 cm, extremely common just below the surface in mid-shore pools. The stiff, flattened tufts, which bear opposite branches, are composed of stubby limy segments. *Jania rubens* **2** is likewise calcareous and segmented, but only 2-5 cm, rose-pink and evenly forking. Its dense tufts occur on other seaweeds, mainly in the south. Two ubiquitous calcareous algae, which look rather like lichens, form crusts on rocks and stones: *Lithothamnion lenormandii* **3** favours shade (e.g. on rocks under *Fucus*) and exposed shores, and is thin and reddish-violet with a white margin and fluted edge, while *Lithophyllum incrustans* **4** is paler, knobbly, up to 1 cm thick and avoids shade.

Rocks in the splash zone show a clear zonation of lichens; grey above, orange, and black below. Highest is *Ramalina siliquosa* **5**, greenish-grey, brittle and tufted. *Lecanora atra* **6** also forms grey cracked crusts with black patches above high water mark. Next comes *Xanthoria parietina* **7**, whose distinctive bright orange foliose crusts differ from another orange lichen, *Caloplaca marina* **8**, in being easily detached from the rock. *Verrucaria maura* **9** forms the black zone on rocks around high water mark, and is often mistaken for oil. *Lichina pygmaea* **10** and *L. confinis* are tufted black lichens, superficially like small *Pelvetia* (p. 32). *L. confinis* extends down to mean high water mark and is found above *L. pygmaea*, which is larger and more tolerant of very exposed conditions.

Plants of muddy shores

At very low tides on quiet, muddy shores great expanses of **eel-grass** *Zostera marina* **1** may be exposed. It has long, flat leaves shaped like lollipop sticks, up to 20 cm long and 5-10 mm wide, but its flowers are green and inconspicuous. In winter, eel-grass beds are an important source of food for wintering brent geese, in particular. Eel-grasses have much broader leaves than **spiral tasselweed** *Ruppia cirrhosa* **2**, which is found in pools in saltmarshes and in slow-flowing ditches of brackish water. With its thread-like leaves and coiled fruit-stalks it is easily recognised.

Much the commonest true grass to be found on bare mud at low tide mark is **cordgrass** *Spartina anglica* **3**, perhaps the best example of a wholly new species to have evolved in recent times. It is the fertile product of a sterile hybrid that formed between the native *S. maritima* and the introduced *S. alterniflora* in Southampton water in the 1870s. It is a vigorous coloniser of bare mud, and has transformed the coastal scene in many places. **Glasswort** *Salicornia europaea* **4** favours similar sites, but is an annual with fleshy leaves, fused and surrounding the stem. In autumn whole patches may turn red or purple, colouring the shore. It is collected and eaten as samphire (which is in truth a quite different plant), particularly along the Norfolk coast.

3

4

Saltmarsh plants

In estuaries where wave action is limited and where silt is brought down by rivers, saltmarshes are formed, between tide marks. They have a characteristic vegetation of plants able to withstand both regular flooding and the salt in the water.

All the plants on this plate have pink or purple flowers and are common on muddy saltmarshes. **Sea aster** *Aster tripolium* **1** (daisy family, Compositae) has fleshy oval leaves at the bottom of the stem, narrower leaves further up, and loose clusters of flowers with yellow centres (disc florets) and variable numbers of violet rays (actually florets, not petals) around them. Sometimes there are no ray florets at all. On grazed marshes it is much favoured by rabbits, and so is often found on rocks and cliffs as well, out of their reach. **Sea lavender** *Limonium vulgare* **2** (Plumbaginaceae) is not related to true lavender, but has vaguely similar flowers, on the tips of curved, one-sided branches, producing a flat-topped head. Sometimes it turns great expanses of marsh into fields of lavender in July. **Greater sea-spurrey** *Spergularia media* **3** (pink family, Caryophyllaceae) is a sprawling perennial with 5-petalled, pink-purple flowers and whorls of leaves like miniature, fleshy pine-needles. Its annual relative, lesser sea-spurrey *S. marina* has smaller pinker flowers and is usually found nearer the top of the marsh. Both have larger flowers than **sea milkwort** *Glaux maritima* **4** (primrose family, Primulaceae), which has creeping, rather woody stems, with opposite pairs of small leaves, each with a tiny pink flower at its base.

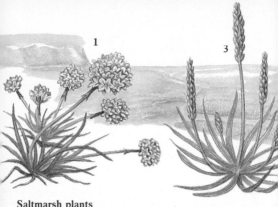

Saltmarsh plants

The plants on these two pages are characteristically found in the middle reaches of saltmarshes, and form together a community known to botanists by the uninspiring name of 'general saltmarsh'. Though not grasses, the first three species do have grass-like leaves, but all are fleshy and broader. The leaves of **thrift** *Armeria maritima* **1** (sea-lavender family, Plumbaginaceae) are narrow and one-veined. The flower heads are very distinctive, with their 5-petalled pink flowers; the heads persist in fruit. Thrift, though common on saltmarshes, is also found on sea-cliffs, and like sea campion (p. 66) also grows on mountain tops, favoured presumably by its cushion-like growth form. **Sea arrow-grass** *Triglochin maritima* **2** (Juncaginaceae) has a long spike of tiny, 3-petalled, greenish flowers, whereas the superficially similar **sea**

plantain *Plantago maritima* **3** (Plantaginaceae) has a much denser spike of 4-petalled flowers, with a ring of yellow anthers when in flower. Sea plantain has veined leaves in contrast to the unveined ones of the arrowgrass. **Sea poa** *Puccinellia maritima* **4** (grass family, Gramineae) grows only in saltmarshes and is best distinguished from the widespread red fescue *Festuca rubra* and creeping bent *Agrostis stolonifera*, which commonly grow with it, by its keeled leaves—run your fingers along the leaves to feel the bump at the tip.

2   4

Plants of the strandline

Sandy shores are found only on exposed coasts, where wave action prevents mud settling; below the high tide mark here no plants can obtain a sure foothold, but just above the strandline are found these four, the first three of which are members of the goosefoot family (Chenopodiaceae) and have tiny green flowers. **Spear-leaved orache** *Atriplex hastata* **1** is an untidy straggling annual with triangular leaves; sometimes the whole plant turns bright red. Several other oraches may be found here, including the common orache *A. patula*, familiar from gardens. **Sea beet** *Beta vulgaris* subspecies *maritima* **2** is a perennial, with rather thick, deep green, untoothed leaves and often reddish stems. It is the wild subspecies and possible ancestor of all cultivated beets, including sugar beet and mangolds. The third goosefoot family plant here is the **prickly saltwort** *Salsola kali* **3**, which is usually prickly on the tips of the leaves: the name *kali* derives from the Arabic word for alkali (qali)—not the Hindu goddess!—because of the high alkali content of its shoots. With its sharp, narrow, fleshy leaves there is little to confuse it with in this habitat. **Sea rocket** *Cakile maritima* **4** (cabbage family, Cruciferae) is very different, with conspicuous spikes of pale to deep lilac flowers, 4-petalled and maturing to a swollen, egg-shaped fruit. Its greyish, fleshy leaves are deeply lobed, and it flowers from June onwards from the strandline to the foredunes.

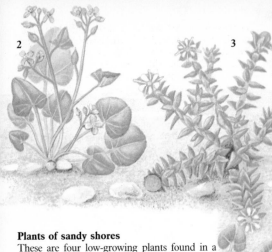

2

3

Plants of sandy shores

These are four low-growing plants found in a range of sandy habitats by the sea. **Buckshorn plantain** *Plantago coronopus* **1** (Plantaginaceae) has greyish, lobed leaves and a typical plantain flower spike; it can be distinguished from sea plantain (pp. 56-7) by its 1-veined leaves—sea plantain's have at least 3 veins. Buckshorn plantain is also found inland, but its typical habitats are dry sandy and clifftop grassland near the sea. **Early scurvy-grass** *Cochlearia danica* **2** (cabbage family, Cruciferae) grows in similar places, and has tiny, pale lilac, 4-petalled flowers from January onwards, with fleshy leaves. It is much smaller than most forms of common scurvy-grass (p. 58) and has oval (not rounded) pods and all its leaves stalked. **Sea sandwort** *Honkenya peploides* **3** (pink family, Caryophyllaceae) is a very fleshy, creeping perennial, with 5-petalled greenish flowers, but the swollen, ball-like yellow fruits are the more conspicuous feature. It very characteristically grows on tiny dunes just above the strand-line, where its ability to keep growing upwards as the sand accumulates enables it to survive, along with sand couch (p. 64). Neither of these plants can form real dunes in the way that marram grass does (p. 64). Sea sandwort also grows on fine shingle, as occasionally does **sea bindweed** *Calystegia soldanella* **4** (Convolvulaceae), which has a creeping stem, large, dark green, fleshy kidney-shaped leaves, and very striking pink flowers, up to 5 cm across and striped white.

Plants of mobile sand: grasses and sedges

Several grasses are commonly found on the front line of the dunes, nearest the sea. They have tough, strong-growing rhizomes and are often planted to aid stabilisation of blown sand. The best known is **marram grass** *Ammophila arenaria* **1** (Gramineae), tall and rough to the touch, with rolled, sharp-tipped leaves, that are painful to walk through. It has a dense, cylindrical spike of large spikelets, each of which has only 1 floret. Marram is the dune-former *par excellence*, maintaining vigorous growth upward for astonishing distances, as the sand accumulates. **Lyme grass** *Leymus* (*Elymus*) *arenarius* **2** and **sand couch grass** *Elymus farctus* (*Agropyron junceiforme*) **3** both have several florets in each spikelet. Lyme grass is much the larger, reaching 2 m, and has broad, hairy leaves; it often grows with marram. Sand couch, however, tends to grow slightly to seaward of both, where the dunes are just forming; it is a bluish plant, rarely over 50 cm high, with hairy leaves. Sea couch *Elymus pycnanthus* is rather larger and has hairless leaves.

Sand sedge *Carex arenaria* **4** (Cyperaceae) is a sedge, but it is a rather grass-like sedge. Sedges have quite different flowers and fruits from grasses, the fruit being a tiny nut. Sand sedge can be recognised from afar by its growth habit: it has a creeping rhizome several cm under the surface of the sand and sends up shoots—a few, stiff, channelled leaves and sometimes a flowering stem—at regular intervals. It is one of the first colonists of blow-outs in the dunes, where the long lines of its shoots stand out on the bare sand.

Plants of shingle

Shingle is one of the most difficult habitats for plants to grow in, for the coarse fragments hold little water and a deep tap-root is a prerequisite. **Yellow horned poppy** *Glaucium flavum* **1** (Papaveraceae) is a most distinctive plant, with its rough leaves, large yellow flowers and extraordinarily long seed-pods, up to 30 cm. It is a tall and rather bushy plant, sometimes found too on waste ground inland. **Sea campion** *Silene maritima* **2** (pink family, Caryophyllaceae) is a much smaller plant, particularly on shingle, where it forms tight, rounded cushions; on cliffs and walls by the sea it tends to be larger and more sprawling. Each white flower has 5 deeply notched petals and a greatly inflated sepal tube. Inland, it is sometimes found on mountains, much as is thrift (p. 56).

The other two species are bushier and more or less shrubby. **Shrubby seablite** *Suaeda vera* **3** (goosefoot family, Chenopodiaceae) is a shrub, one of the few that are truly coastal—sea buckthorn *Hippophaë rhamnoides* with thorny stems, silvery leaves and bright orange berries is really a sand-dune plant. *Suaeda* is a metre or so high and closely resembles annual seablite (p. 58), but the leaves are blunt-tipped. It often forms dense stands, but is only found on the south and east coasts. **Sea kale** *Crambe maritima* **4** (cabbage family, Cruciferae) has a thick woody stem and large, wavy, fleshy leaves; it has the typical four-petalled flowers of its family and ball-like fruits. Sea kale grows on both sandy and shingly shores, mainly in the south.

Plants of sand and shingle

The plants on this plate grow in similar habitats but never together in a geographical sense in Britain. **Sea holly** *Eryngium maritimum* **1** is a plant of south-west Europe, whose range just reaches to south and south-west Britain. It gets its name from the spiny greyish leaves, but it is a member of the carrot family (Umbelliferae) and not a holly. The head of pale blue flowers is rather reminiscent of a teasel. **Oyster plant** *Mertensia maritima* **2** (borage family, Boraginaceae), whose fleshy, blue-grey leaves are said to taste of oysters, is a high northern plant, quite common in places in Scotland, but scarcely reaching even to northern England. It has forgetmenot-like flowers, which open pink and turn blue, and forms creeping mats over shingle.

The other two plants are common and widespread and both have familiar relatives inland. **Sea mayweed** *Tripleurospermum maritimum* **3** (daisy family, Compositae) has

2

feathery leaves and daisy-like flowers; it is more
erect and slightly fleshier than the very similar scent-
less mayweed *T. inodorum*, found on waste ground
inland. **Curled dock** *Rumex crispus* **4** (Polygonaceae)
is often found on shingle banks, but there it is a
distinct subspecies with slightly different fruits and
a distinct ecology. It has long wavy-edged leaves and
green whorls of flowers, turning brown in fruit.

Lower invertebrates: sponges, coelenterates, ctenophores, platyhelminths, nemertines

All animals and plants are built up of cells; the simplest animals are the single-celled protozoa which are abundant in the plankton (p. 12). Sponges are the most primitive multicellular animals, whose 2 layers of cells are rather loosely organised into a hollow structure. Water is drawn in through small inhalant pores, **ostia**, and out via large exhalant **oscula**, by the beating of whip-like **flagella** on the inner cells. The body is strengthened by **spicules** of lime, silica or fibre. The bath sponge is a Mediterranean species; the fibrous skeleton is all that remains but the oscula are clearly visible.

Like sponges, coelenterates are mainly marine. All have a radial symmetry, a hollow body made of 2 well defined cell layers, with a nerve net between (unlike sponges), and a single opening through which matter is both ingested and egested. All have sting cells, which paralyse prey, on tentacles round the mouth. Sea firs (hydroids) are colonies of sedentary polyps, supported by a horny skeleton into which they can retract for protection. The colony reproduces by budding; also special structures, the **vases**,

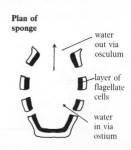

Plan of sponge

water out via osculum

layer of flagellate cells

water in via ostium

bear **medusae**, the planktonic dispersal phase. Jelly-fish (scyphozoans) are large free-swimming medusae with an inconspicuous polyp phase, while sea anemones (anthozoans) have no medusoid phase at all.

Comb jellies (ctenophores) are small transparent planktonic animals similar to coelenterates but lacking sting cells—instead sticky cells trap prey. Beating of combs of tiny iridescent hairs, the **cilia**, in 8 bands causes movement. Flatworms (platyhelminths) have definite head and tail ends, and 3 layers of cells, the middle layer containing muscles and nerves. A ventral **pharynx** helps ingest prey. Unlike flatworms, ribbon or proboscis worms (nemertines) have an anus as well as a mouth, and a **proboscis** housed in a pouch above, and unconnected with the mouth. Most of these animals have planktonic larvae.

Small, colourless worms, pointed at both ends with rather rigid lashing movements, are nematodes—roundworms. They are ubiquitous, but often found in mud under stones and in guts of most fish.

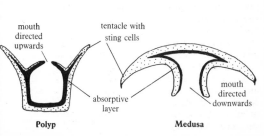

mouth directed upwards

tentacle with sting cells

absorptive layer

mouth directed downwards

Polyp

Medusa

PORIFERA **sponges**

Sponges are very primitive animals, colourful, numerous and easily seen. *Grantia compressa* **1**, *Sycon coronatum* **2** and *Leucosolenia botryoides* **3** are all common purse sponges, white or creamy yellow, with calcareous spicules. *Grantia* has a solitary, smooth vase, 2-5 cm, which hangs from the undersides of overhangs amongst red weeds near low water mark. In *Sycon*, **urn** or **crown sponge**, the rougher vases have a jagged fringe of spicules, several arising from a common stalk, while the small (8 mm long), simple, pale vases of *Leucosolenia* grow like tiny white bananas from a base of branching canals, usually around *Fucus* stipes.

The **boring sponge** *Cliona celata* **4** secretes an acid which enables it to bore numerous tiny holes into the limy shells of scallop, *Venus* and oysters, through which yellow lobes, 2 mm across, can be seen protruding. The last three sponges here have silica spicules, are very common and have similar encrusting, colonial habits. **Breadcrumb sponge** *Halichondria panicea* **5** is frequently green, but may be white or yellow. The incrustation, 1 cm thick, on sheltered rocks and often under wracks, is smooth except for large, raised, regularly spaced pores (oscula) like tiny volcanoes; when pressed water squirts out of these. *Hymeniacidon perleve* **6** is redder and rougher, with more oscula, while *Myxilla incrustans* **7** forms a furrowed, bright orange pad (4 cm thick), with large flush oscula; on rocks, often near muddy sand, or on large crustacea.

Coelenterates Hydrozoans: **sea firs**

Hydroids or sea firs are coelenterates attached
to shells, weeds and rock. Often only the
sheath remains, but the skeleton patterns are
characteristic. *Dynamena* (*Sertularia*) *pumila* **1**
and *Kirchenpaueria* (*Plumularia*) *pinnata* **2**,
both up to 12 mm, are very common, especially on *Fucus* and rocks, but the trans
parent grey, often unbranched colonies of the
former appear serrated due to their oppositely
paired polyps. Randomly placed capsules are
the reproductive 'vases'. *Kirchenpaueria* is
cream, and its regularly alternating,
jointed side-branches have cups on one side only,
giving it a feathery look. Vases occur on either
side of the main stalk. *Obelia geniculata* **3**, to
4 cm, has short, alternating branches with
terminal polyps in bell-shaped cups, giving it
a zig-zag shape. Hoops round the stalk make
it flexible; very common on brown weeds.
Laomedea (*Campanularia*) *flexuosa* **4**, to 2 cm,

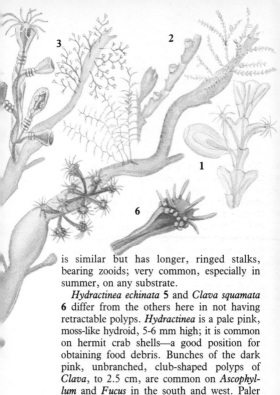

is similar but has longer, ringed stalks, bearing zooids; very common, especially in summer, on any substrate.

Hydractinea echinata 5 and *Clava squamata* 6 differ from the others here in not having retractable polyps. *Hydractinea* is a pale pink, moss-like hydroid, 5-6 mm high; it is common on hermit crab shells—a good position for obtaining food debris. Bunches of the dark pink, unbranched, club-shaped polyps of *Clava*, to 2.5 cm, are common on *Ascophyllum* and *Fucus* in the south and west. Paler tentacles are scattered over the polyps.

75

COELENTERATES Scyphozoans: **jellyfish**

Jellyfish are large coelenterates which may be seen in clear deep water, e.g. harbours, swimming with pulsating bell and trailing tentacles; but are frequently stranded by the receding tide, especially in late summer. The **common jellyfish** *Aurelia aurita* **1** is transparent except for 4 mauve crescent-shaped reproductive organs around the mouth, which is extended in all jellyfish into 4 fleshy lobes. The saucer, up to 30 cm in diameter, is flattened and fringed by short tentacles. The **compass jellyfish** *Chrysaora hysoscella* **2** is 50cm in diameter, cream with brown radiating patches on the brown-edged umbrella; the 4 trailing frilly mouth lappets are longer than the 24 tentacles. These can give a harmful sting—hence its other name 'sea nettle'. Mainly found in the south and west. The violet-blue *Cyanea lamarckii* **3** has 4 frilly mouth lappets which are shorter than the very long tentacles arising in 8 bunches from the marginal lobes; a mainly eastern species. The yellow *C. capillata* occurs in the south-west. Both can sting. Also occurring in the south and west is the largest British jellyfish *Rhizostoma pulmo* **4**, which may be 60cm or more and has a globular, apple-green bell fringed with small purple lobes but no tentacles. The mouth lappets are fused to form a mesh through which water and prey pass.

76

77

COELENTERATES Anthozoans: **sea anemones**

Sea anemones or Anthozoa are sessile coelenterates and occur only as polyps. The commonest is the **beadlet** *Actinia equina* **1**, which can be very numerous on rocks and in pools from midshore down, even on very exposed shores. Its smooth column is often brick-red, but can be green or cherry-red with green spots, and carries about 200 retractable, 2-cm long tentacles. When exposed, the beadlet is a flat-topped blob of jelly, 3 cm high, with 24 bright blue spots round the edge of the mouth disc **1a**. In sunny pools, on laminarians or in crevices, but not on the east coast, can be seen the graceful, tapered tentacles of the **opelet** or **snakelocks** *Anemonia sulcata* **2**. Its 150 or more unretractable tentacles, 5 to 12 cm long, can give a nasty sting, and are khaki or green with iridescent violet tips. The column is smooth and wide-based, as is that of the **plumose anemone** *Metridium senile* **3**, a large, mainly sublittoral anemone sometimes found low on the shore under overhangs, in clefts or on pier pilings. The 8-cm column and the bushy crown of very numerous delicate tentacles can be beige, cream or pink. The **dahlia anemone** *Tealia felina* **4**, though common, can be hard to see, since sand and shell particles adhere to the vertical grey lines of warts on the 5-cm, crimson, grey or green column **4a**. It is attached by a very broad base, 10 cm in diameter, in shade in pools and under kelp, low on shore. Its 80 stubby, translucent and grey-banded tentacles open exposing a flat oval disc with the mouth at its centre.

COELENTERATES Anthozoans: **sea anemones** and Ctenophores: **comb jellies**

Daisy anemone *Actinocereus pedunculatus* **1** and *Sagartia elegans* **2** are flower-like with vase-shaped columns, usually wedged deep in cracks in pools or half-buried on stones in mud near low water. Both have sticky, retractable, often grey-spotted columns, and emit white stinging threads (acontia) when disturbed. *Actinocereus* has 300 tentacles, is pale and mainly in the south-west, while *Sagartia* is smaller, with fewer crimson, brown or white tentacles and a rusty body; more widespread. The **gem anemone** *Bunodactis verrucosa* **3** favours well-lit pools in the south and west only. Its pinkish column is studded with 6 rows of white warts and 48 banded tentacles. The **cloak anemone** *Adamsia palliata* **4** is commensal on shells occupied by hermit crabs. The basal disc, beige with red spots, covers the shell; purple acontia and 500 white tentacles surround the aperture. In sheltered gullies at ELWS grows the colonial soft coral *Alcyonium digitatum* **5**, to 20 cm, known as **dead men's fingers**, which the soft, flesh-coloured lobes resemble; each has many polyps with 8 tentacles. Two transparent planktonic comb-jellies (Ctenophores), may be stranded in late summer. **Sea gooseberry** *Pleurobrachia pileus* **6** is oval, to 1.5 cm, with 8 ribs bearing combs and 2 long retractile tentacles. *Beroë cucumis* **7**, 5 cm, lacks tentacles.

4

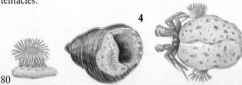

PLATYHELMINTHS **flatworms**

Though simple in structure, the Platyhelminths or flatworms are the first group to show bilateral symmetry. These free-living worms are related to parasitic flukes and tapeworms. Their flattened, leaf-like bodies are suited to flowing smoothly under stones. They have a mouth on the lower surface, no anus, are hermaphrodite, and, though inconspicuous, are nevertheless widespread and abundant.

Procerodes littoralis **1** is common under stones on the upper half of the shore where there is fresh water seepage. Its grey-brown streaked body is 5 mm long, has a rounded tail, 3 main gut branches, which are often visible, two eyes and two stumpy 'horns'.

Also common, but lacking tentacles, is *Leptoplana tremellaris* **2**, 2.5 cm long, with a beige, speckled oval body, black eye spots and a dark nerve area at the front. Found from mid-shore down under stones, it can also swim. *Oligocladus sanguinolentus* **3**, 1 cm long, is semi-transparent with a creamy body marked with rusty patches. It has many eyes and a pair of pointed tentacles. Much larger, and confined to the south-west, is *Prostheceraeus vittatus* **4**, whose pale yellow, leaf-like body is 3 cm long; it is patterned with dark longitudinal lines, and has a wavy margin, pointed tail, and two long tentacles. This impressive flatworm can be found amongst laminarians or under stones in muddy gravel.

NEMERTINES **ribbon worms**

The nemertines, the bootlace or proboscis worms, are a group of soft, flexible, mostly marine worms, easily able to change shape from coiled knots of jelly to long thin threads. Though closely related to flatworms (p. 82), they have an anus and a long evertible proboscis, which can be shot out of an opening in front of the mouth to catch prey, such as annelid worms, and pass it to the mouth. Their movements are a slow wriggling, caused by forward-moving waves along the body. Although common, they are easily overlooked as they normally live under stones in muddy sand and gravel. The **bootlace** *Lineus longissimus* **1** is the longest British invertebrate, commoner in the north. Its elastic, shiny, brown-black body, though usually coiled under stones

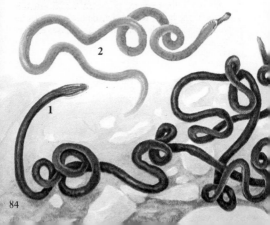

low on shore, can be extended to an amazing 5 m or more. It has many indistinct eyes and, if broken, it can regenerate. The **red ribbon worm** *L. ruber* **2**, to 20 cm, is shown here with everted proboscis. It is flattened and reddish, though paler below, with a 'neck' and 2 lines of eyes either side of the head; common under stones in gravel, especially in estuaries. *Tubulanus annulatus* **3**, 12-50 cm, is distinctive, with a plaid of white lines marking its rounded, rusty-brown body. It lacks eyes, has a 'neck' and tapering tail, and secretes tubes of mucus under stones low on shore. Common among laminarian holdfasts and in shingle is the pink ribbon worm *Amphiporus lactifloreus* **4**, 7 cm, whose pale pink body has 2 darker spots at the base of the head, a 'neck', a blunt tail and a translucent line down the back where the retracted proboscis lies. Everted, it is as long as the body, with stylets on the end. Eyes lie in two rows, either side of the head, and in two clusters in the middle.

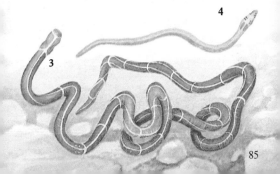

Annelids

All annelids, whether polychaetes (marine bristle worms), earthworms or leeches, differ from the preceding worms in having cylindrical bodies divided by **septa** into repeated segments. Bristle worms possess side-lobes, the **parapodia**, from all but the front two and end segments, which bear tiny bristles or **chaetae**. They are a very diverse group, abundant if secretive, and are important food for waders, fish

Dorsal view: *Neanthes diversicolor*

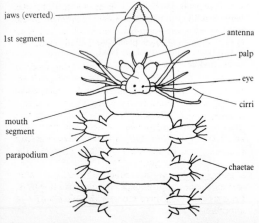

jaws (everted)

1st segment

antenna

palp

eye

cirri

mouth
segment

parapodium

chaetae

and bait for anglers. They fall into 2 groups, the errant which move freely under stones and weed or burrowing in sand, and the sedentary which live permanently in burrows or tubes for protection.

Errant polychaetes crawl with their prominent parapodia and swim with undulating body movements; some, such as the paddleworms, have efficient expanded parapodial paddles. Most are predators with distinct heads bearing sense organs for detecting prey, and often powerful jaws borne on a **proboscis** which is rapidly everted to snatch prey.

Sedentary polychaetes have many modifications to tube dwelling; they no longer have use for elaborate sense organs or jaws, parapodia are reduced, bristles being modified to grip tube sides. Movement in the tube is by earthworm-like waves of contraction. Gills, often modified from parapodial **cirri**, are enlarged.

They need special tentacles for collecting food; in *Amphitrite*, a deposit feeder, sticky threads pick up debris which is moved by tiny hairs, the **cilia**, along grooves to the mouth while cilia on the crown of suspension feeders like *Sabella* create currents so that particles are trapped and later sorted. The crown also acts as gills. Other tube worms, *Arenicola* and *Capitella*, feed by ingesting sand and removing the organic part in the gut.

Most polychaetes release their sex cells into water and the larvae are planktonic. In some errant worms, prior to spawning there are considerable changes in appearance.

ANNELIDS **scale worms**

Scale worms are polychaetes, oval and flattened, with plate-like protective and respiratory scales, the elytra, on their upper surface. They are active and fragile, and can easily lose scales when handled. *Harmothoë impar* **1**, is 1-3 cm long, completely covered by 15 pairs of overlapping, knobbly khaki scales, sometimes phosphorescent, with a yellowish central spot, and fringed with hairs. It has long (2 cm) anal cirri, and is common below midshore under weed and stones. *Lagisca extenuata* **2** also has 15 pairs of scales, marbled brown with grey or red markings, and a clear spot in the centre, but the tail is naked and ends in 2 long anal cirri. This large worm, 3-4 cm, is common in low shore rock cracks and under stones, especially in the south. Twelve pairs of kidney-shaped, overlapping, buff or brown elytra cover the whole body of *Lepidonotus squamatus* **3**. Its rather stiff body is 1.5-3 cm long, of uniform width, and has a reticulate pattern; it occurs in similar places to *Harmothoë*.

Not uncommon on sand into which it can rapidly burrow is the very large, grey or beige *Sthenelais boa* **4**, whose 156 pairs of overlapping scales cover the whole body, save for two long anal cirri. The **sea mouse** *Aphrodite aculeata* **5** is 15 cm long, and, though really sublittoral, can be found at extreme low water under sand, or washed up at the strandline. Its elytra act as gills and are hidden by a protective mat of dull brown hairs, but the lateral chaetae are iridescent green and gold.

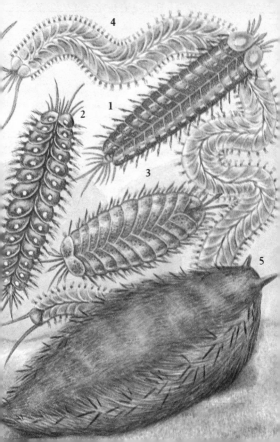

ANNELIDS **ragworms and** *Glycera*

Ragworms are active, omnivorous predators, whose large heads are endowed with 2 short antennae, 4 eyes, feelers and an evertible proboscis armed with 2 black-tipped jaws. They are much collected for angling bait and most burrow in soft substrates or lie under stones. The **king rag** *Neanthes* (*Nereis*) *virens* **1**, 20-40 cm or more, is a splendid pale green worm, iridescent with purple and yellow, as thick as a finger and with paddle-like lobes extending from the parapodia; it has powerful jaws. It lives in mucus-lined burrows in wet mud under stones low on shore, in which it creates respiratory currents by undulations of its body. Like *Neanthes virens*, *Nereis pelagica* **2**, to 10 cm, is commonest in the north, but this bronze worm with greenish parapodia lives on rocky shores, amongst weed and shells, while *Neanthes* (*Nereis*) *diversicolor* **3**, to 10 cm, is abundant in sandy mud, especially in estuaries, on the lower shore. It has very small antennae and a distinct red line down its back. *Perinereis cultrifera* **4**, 10-25 cm, is common in gravelly mud, among weed and under stones. It is iridescent khaki with reddish parapodia and dorsal line, a tapering tail, and 2 groups of teeth behind eyebrow-like jaws. *Glycera convoluta* **5**, 3-9 cm, is not a ragworm, though it has black jaws. Transparent pale pink and tapering at both ends, this round, slender worm has 4 tiny antennae on a short stub and a bulb-shaped proboscis tipped with 4 teeth. It is very common low on sandy shores and twists and coils vigorously if disturbed.

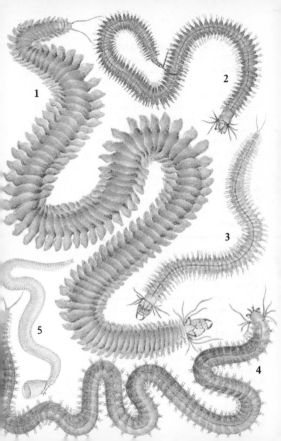

ANNELIDS **rock, cat and paddle worms**

The **rockworm** *Eunice harassi* **1**, 15-20 cm, is reddish-brown, rather earthworm-like, and found on south-western shores in crevices and under stones. It has 5 yellow-ringed antennae, the middle one longest, 2 eyes, black lower jaw and toothed, rasping upper jaw, conspicuous feathery red gills, and 4 tail bristles. *Nephthys caeca* **2** and the **cat worm** *N. hombergii* **3** are flattened, pearly worms with no visible eyes and a single tail bristle. Much used as bait, they burrow in sand and coarse mud below mid-shore. Both wriggle actively and can swim. *N. caeca*, to 25 cm, is larger, with soft yellow bristles; *N. hombergii*, 10 cm, has a wide grey line on its back and darker, shorter bristles; abundant even in estuaries. The paddleworms, **green leaf worm** *Eulalia viridis* **4** and *Anaitides maculata* **5** are so called because of leaf-like parapodial extensions, which permit active and graceful swimming. Superficially like rag-worms, they lack jaws and catch prey with the long everted proboscis. *Eulalia*, 5-15 cm, has 2 eyes, 5 antennae and 4 pairs of feelers on a blunt head. It is common crawling on rocks, in crevices and under stones and weed at low tide, especially in early summer, when it lays round green 1 cm egg capsules which hang from *Fucus* by threads. The less common *Anaitides*, 15 cm, has brown spots or bars across each segment.

5

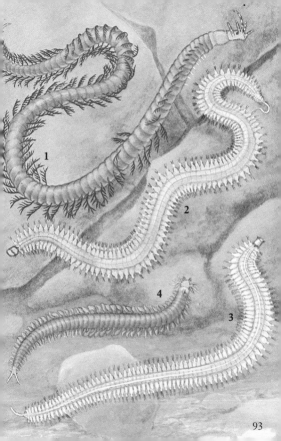

1

2

4

3

93

ANNELIDS **calcareous tube worms**
The worms on pp. 96-99 are sedentary, living in a
burrow or tube; those on this plate live in a dull white
calcareous tube cemented to shells, algae and rocks.
They withdraw calcium from the water, secrete it as
calcium carbonate mixed with mucus, and mould it
into a tube, whose shape is characteristic for each
species. The worms are free in the tubes and, when
disturbed, can withdraw into them, closing the end
with a plug modified from a tentacle.

Spirorbis spirorbis **1** is abundant, especially on
Fucus vesiculosus and *F. serratus*, the smooth, spirally
coiled tubes, 2 mm across, growing clockwise; its
green gills protrude when covered by the tide. *S.*

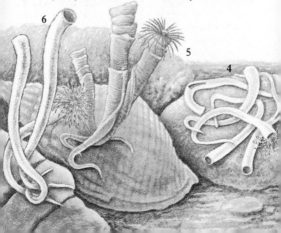

tridentatus **2**, found on rocks, is similar but with 3 ridges down the tube and creamy gills, while *Janua pagenstecheri* has anti-clockwise coils. Common on stones and shells in twisted aggregates low on shore, *Pomatoceros triqueter* **3** is larger (5 cm); its triangular tube has a keel which ends as a tooth at the opening. Its gills are barred red and white. The smaller, entwined, unkeeled tubes of *Hydroides norvegica* **4**, though sublittoral, are often cast up on shells and stones. *Serpula vermicularis* **5**, to 8 cm, and *Protula tubularia* **6**, to 10 cm, have more upright, often entwined tubes, wider at the open end; though sublittoral, they are commonly cast ashore. *Serpula* has red gills and its pink or green-tinged tube has growth rings, while *Protula* is smooth, white and lacks a plug. *Filograna implexa* **7** forms colonies, up to 15 square cm, of thin twisting tubes low on shore; often cast up.

ANNELIDS **worms making tubes of sand, mud or mucus**

The **fan** or **peacock worm** *Sabella penicillus* **1** and *Branchiomma vesiculosum* **2** build tubes which protrude from sandy or muddy flats, very low on shore. *Sabella* is dull green, to 15 cm, with 8-45 feathery, greenish-banded tentacles, 3 cm long, arising from 2 lobes and making a beautiful, funnel-shaped crown. This can rapidly be retracted into the smooth, flexible tube, 30 cm long, which projects about 10 cm, and to which fine particles of mud adhere. *Branchiomma* is orange and has a tougher tube, 25 cm long and protruding 2.5 cm, with large sand and shell particles attached to the base. The 18-24 finely feathered tentacles do not arise from lobes, but are darker at the base, and the 2 central have a distinct dark spot at the tip; common in the south and southwest. The **sand mason** *Lanice conchilega* **3** builds a 30 cm long tube, encrusted with shell and sand, which protrudes stiffly to 4 cm, and is fringed with bristles round the opening. The brownish worm, to 25 cm long, has pale pink tentacles, 3 pairs of branching red gills, and a broad red line on its back; common in sand below midshore. The related *Amphitrite johnstoni* **4** and *Polymnia nebulosa* **5** secrete fragile mucous tubes under stones low on the shore, with only the tangled crown of sticky, writhing tentacles and red gills exposed. Both have plump, tapering bodies; *Amphitrite* is 18 cm, buff with pale brown tentacles, its tube a hole in the sand, while *Polymnia* is 15 cm, orange with white markings and pink or white tentacles.

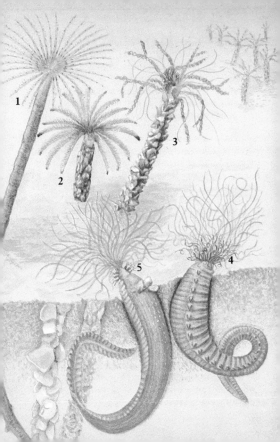

ANNELIDS **worms making tubes in rock and of mucus**
On rocks and boulders in sand, colonial *Sabellaria* species **1** build hardened tubes, 5 mm in diameter, of large sand grains, resembling a honeycomb of sandstone. The reddish-brown worm, is 2-3 cm, has a distinct purple tube-plug and short tentacles at the head end, prominent parapodia in the middle, and a thin bent tail; common low on shore on beaches of moderate exposure and in estuaries. Species of *Polydora* **2** live in minute, mucus-lined, U-shaped tubes 1-2 mm in diameter, which they bore by dissolving limestone, shale, or shells, usually in shallow pools. Both ends of the tube are extended by mud and mucus and protrude 1 cm or so out of cracks, their presence being shown by two flailing, food-seeking, thread-like tentacles from one end. **Red threads** *Cirriformia tentaculata* **3** is a flame-coloured worm, to 15 cm, pointed at both ends, with two bunches of coiling, red feeding tentacles arising from the 6th or 7th segment, and similar thread-like gills from most other body segments. It is a detritus feeder, very common in mucous tubes under stones in gravelly sand and dirty mud on the lower shore, but rare in the north, where it is replaced by the smaller *Cirratulus cirratus*, which has fewer tentacles. Also secreting a fragile mucous burrow in black (anaerobic) mud or sand is the small, smooth round, blood-red worm *Capitella capitata* **4**, 2-10 cm, which has an unarmed proboscis and a swollen front end—rather like an earthworm; it is common on the midshore and below.

lugworm and worms in sand

The coiled worm casts which are such a characteristic feature of the lower half of sandy or muddy flats are produced by lugworms, the commonest of which is *Arenicola marina* **1**. Abundant and sought after as bait, lugworms make L-shaped burrows, held in shape by a thin mucous secretion. Pumping body movements create a water current which passes from the rear end forward over the 13 pairs of red gills (thus supplying oxygen), and then over the head and out at the front of the burrow. The effect is to loosen and disturb the

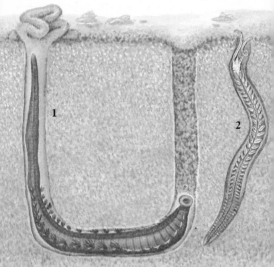

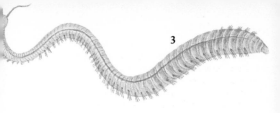

sand above the extrusible, unarmed proboscis which continuously ingests particles. Organic matter is digested and waste material is voided from the upright limb of the tube every 40 minutes or so, after which the worm returns to the burrow base. The cast is about 15 cm from a depression in the sand which marks the entrance. The lugworm is wrinkled, green or black, 15-20 cm, soft and fat, except for a narrower, firm tail which lacks appendages.

Nerine cirratulus **2** is a thin, greenish-blue worm, 5-7 cm, which is common in clean sand and gravel on the mid and lower shore all round Britain. It makes a mucous burrow. The head is pointed and two long, thin, flexible palps, each with a ciliated groove for food collection, are often folded back and hidden amongst the red gills which flank the body.

Also long and slender, but lacking any head appendages, is *Scoloplos armiger* **3**, 5-12 cm long and 2 mm broad, whose orange body tapers and ends in two tail threads. The bristles towards the end point upwards across the back. Common in midshore sand or mud, this rather inactive worm burrows without actually making a tube, and in this respect is reminiscent of the errant polychaetes.

Molluscs

There is a huge variety of molluscs, but although they do live in freshwater and on land, most are marine. The several classes look very different but all have a muscular foot, a **mantle** which secretes a protective shell (which may only be present in the larval phase) and gills in the mantle cavity. The shell is mainly calcium carbonate and limestone rocks are often remains of millions of years of the deposit of the shells. Gastropods (snails) and chitons have a single shell, that of the primitive limpet-like chitons with 8 articulating plates. The gastropod shell is spiral (usually right-handed as viewed from above, left-handed ones are rare) around a central column, the **columella**, which in some snails (e.g. *Gibbula umbilicalis*) is hollow, and forms the **umbilicus**. When exposed or disturbed, the body can be completely withdrawn into the shell which is closed by a horny **operculum** (except in limpets). Snails glide on the foot, eased by mucous secretions. The head carries two tentacles with eyes and a **radula** or tongue which rasps algae in the herbivores, but in carnivores like whelks, has fewer, larger teeth at the end of a flexible snout or **proboscis**.

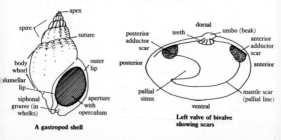

A gastropod shell

Left valve of bivalve showing scars

Creatures of delicate beauty, the sea slugs are protected in the absence of a shell by being either unpalatable, or armed with sting cells 'borrowed' from coelenterates, or by ejecting a slimy fluid when disturbed. They have 2 pairs of tentacles and, lacking a mantle cavity, have external gills or **cerata**. Most snails and slugs have planktonic larvae but many lay egg ribbons on weed and rocks in spring.

Lamellibranchs or bivalves have 2 flattened shells or **valves** held together at the hinge, which may be toothed, by a ligament. The valves are closed by two transverse **adductor** muscles, and contain the body—mainly a compressed foot used for digging—and a pair of large ciliated gills which not only collect oxygen from the water which is drawn over them, but also filter food. Apart from the swimming scallops, bivalves are inactive, either attached by **byssus** threads to rocks, or buried, and all are filter or deposit feeders. Often only the empty shells are found, with concentric growth lines like tree rings on the outside, the **umbo** being the oldest part. The inner layer of some shells is mother-of-pearl, and pearls are formed when the mantle lays down the same material round some foreign particle. Inside, apart from the adductor scars, the **pallial line** marks the attachment of the mantle edge to the shell. Often the two mantle flaps are joined except for an inhalent and exhalent opening (and one for the foot). In deep burrowers, with their flat valves, these may be extended into siphons which can be retracted.

Cephalopods are the most advanced molluscs, with well developed brains (they can learn) and 2 complex focusing eyes which rival those of vertebrates. Their foot is modified to form an exhalent funnel through which water is forced for jet propulsion.

MOLLUSCS Polyplacophorans: **chitons**

Chitons are primitive, bilaterally symmetrical molluscs with flattened oval bodies and no tentacles or eyes. They browse slowly over rocks and stones near low water and below. A shell of 8 overlapping, transverse plates gives flexibility to adjust to rock contours, to which chitons adhere closely and inconspicuously, using their broad, limpet-like foot. In storms, or if disturbed, they can curl into a ball. The mantle forms a fringe right round the shell (seen from above) called the girdle, which usually contains spicules. Gills are found down both sides between the mantle and the side of the foot.

The **coat-of-mail chiton** *Lepidopleurus asellus* **1** is very common from extreme low water and below, and is about 1.5 cm long by 1 cm broad, with smooth, shiny, ash-coloured flattened plates, which have wavy lateral edges. The narrow mantle is not variegated and there are 8-13 gills. The commonest chiton, found on rocks and under stones from midshore and below, is *Lepidochitona cinereus* **2**, which measures 1.5 by 0.7 cm. The plates are keeled, dull red, brown or green, and notched at the sides; the girdle is broad, granular and variegated, and there are 16-19 gills. *Tonicella rubra* **3**, 1.7 by 0.9 cm, is distinguished by its reddish, shiny shell, narrow granular, red and white marked girdle and 10-15 gills. Its plates also have notched edges. *Acanthochitona crinitus* **4** is narrower, with rough, granular yellow or brown plates and 9 pairs of bristly tufts down each side; it is common in the south and west.

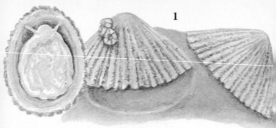

Molluscs Gastropods: **limpets**

Limpets have conical shells, no operculum, and adhere closely to rocks by the suction of the large muscular foot. The **common limpet** *Patella vulgata* **1**, abundant on the upper half of all rocky shores, especially exposed ones, settles where the larvae are not brushed off by weed, and browses when covered by the tide on encrusting algae and sporelings, using its rasping radula. Limpets return 'home' to the same site, where either the shell or the rock (whichever is softer) becomes ground to match the other, thus ensuring, when clamped down, a water-tight fit against both buffeting waves and dehydration. The shell is dull, grey, tall and ribbed, to 7 cm long, with a scalloped edge, and often barnacle-encrusted.

The attractive and unmistakeable **blue-rayed limpet** *Patina pellucida* **2** is common on *Laminaria*, on which it feeds. Young shells are fragile, smooth, honey-coloured and semi-transparent, with 3 or more rows of iridescent kingfisher-blue spots running from apex to margin. They are found mainly on stipes and fronds. As they age, the limpets (2 by 1.5 cm), now on the holdfasts, become opaque and greenish and the rays fade. There is a ring of gills around the foot. The **white tortoiseshell limpet** *Acmaea virginea* **3** is also found amongst *Laminaria* and below. Its smooth, flattened creamy-white shell (to 1.3 cm) has buff markings and its apex is well forward. The **tortoiseshell** *A. tessulata* **4**, is a northern species, similar but larger (to 2.5 cm), with a more delicate brown shell, marked with a reddish pattern like tortoiseshell; found beneath stones at low water. Both have a single gill.

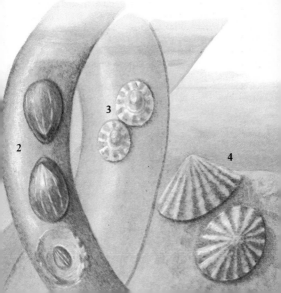

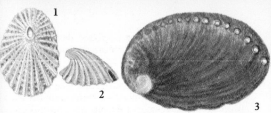

MOLLUSCS Gastropods **limpets**

The first three limpets here have 2 gills over which a current is drawn, and then ejected from a siphon via perforations on the shell, well away from the entering current. The **keyhole limpet** *Diodora apertura* **1** (to 4 cm) occurs low on shores in the south and south-west. Its greyish conical ribbed shell has a hole at the apex, and the foot clearly overlaps the margin. The **slit limpet** *Emarginula reticulata* **2** is about half the size, with a creamy, ribbed shell, slit at the front, and with the apex slightly leaning. It occurs on stones and shells very low on the shore. Although the **ormer** (from 'oreille de mer') *Haliotis tuberculata* **3** is only found in the Channel Islands, its large (to 8 cm), flattened spiral shell, rimmed with small holes and lined with mother-of-pearl, is easily identified in shell collections. As the shell grows, new apertures form and the old ones close up.

Two more advanced gastropods, not closely related to these three, have adopted the limpet form. The **slipper limpet** *Crepidula fornicata* **4** was introduced with oysters from the USA last century, and is now common on oyster and mussel beds on the south and east coasts, competing with them for food. The adults, sedentary filter-feeders like bivalves, grow in piles of 2-12. They are hermaphrodite, but the oldest at the bottom of the pile are ♀, the youngest (at the top) are ♂. The shell is oval, 4 by 2.5 cm, grey or khaki with reddish markings, a coiled apex, and a white ledge inside, making it look like a slipper. The round white shell of the **Chinaman's hat** *Calyptraea chinensis* **5**, up to 2 cm across and 7 mm high, has a central glossy apex and a sloping ledge beneath. Found near low water on stones and shells in the south-west, it is another filter-feeder, and is also found in chains.

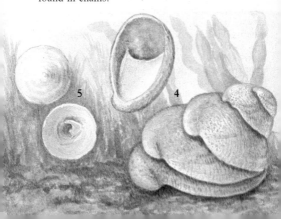

5

4

Molluscs Gastropods: **topshells**

Topshells are attractive conical shells of rocky shores. All browse algae and most have a hollow central column (the umbilicus) and are lined with mother-of-pearl. These species of *Gibbula* show zonation in their preferred position on the shore. The **flat** or **purple topshell** *G. umbilicalis* **1** is the highest, and common around mid-tide level amongst *Fucus serratus* in the south-west. Its shell is 1.2 cm high, greyish with broad purplish lines, and compressed and slightly convex in outline, with an obvious umbilicus. The **grey topshell** or **silver tommy** *G. cineraria* **2** is less flattened, with 7 whorls and very fine purplish markings on a grey ground. It is very common from mid-tide level down. Occupying the lowest zone on the shore, and fairly common in the south and west, is *G. magus* **3**. Its large (2.3 cm high), strong, flattened shell is pale yellow with pink markings, a bumpy surface on the 8 whorls, and a conspicuous umbilicus. The **thick topshell** *Monodonta lineata* **4** is found above *G. umbilicalis* but only in the south-west. Grey-green with a purple herringbone pattern, it has a tooth-like process on the opening and is often worn at its apex. Also about 2.5 cm high is the **painted topshell** *Calliostoma zizyphinum* **5** with its straight-sided, broad-based, pointed buff shell with reddish streaks. It is found at extreme low water in crevices and under ledges. The **pheasant shell** *Tricolia pullus* **6** has a glossy brown, mottled shell, taller (8 mm) than broad, a white operculum, and is often found amongst red weeds in pools at low water in the south and west.

MOLLUSCS Gastropods: **periwinkles**

Periwinkles *Littorina* are the commonest snails of the rocky shore, and the four species show distinct zonation. **Small periwinkle** *L. neritoides* **1** is found in crevices in the splash zone on exposed shores. Effectively terrestrial, it breathes with lungs, feeds on lichens, but still relies on very high tides to distribute its eggs. The smooth, fragile, pointed shell (to 5 mm) is blue-black with a hazy bloom. The **rough periwinkle** *L. saxatilis* **2** is variable in size (to 1.2 cm), colour (red, cream, green, orange, striped), and texture, but is always rough to the touch. Its tentacles have 2 dark longitudinal lines, there are well-marked whorls, and the outer rim of the opening meets the body whorl at right angles (obliquely in *L. littorea*). Found around high water mark, it has a modified lung and the ♀ gives birth to tiny shelled young, like sand grains. Small snails may cluster in dead barnacle shells. In the midshore, on bladder and egg wrack, is the smooth, compressed **flat periwinkle** *L. littoralis* **3**, to 1 cm high, orange, yellow or green with a wide shell opening, and laying a gelatinous eggmass on weed. The dull grey-black shell, to 3.5 cm high, of the **edible periwinkle** *L. littorea* **4** is common in low pools. It has black-banded tentacles, a striped foot and dark lines on the pointed shell. The **banded chink** *Lacuna vincta* **5**, 1 cm high, occurs on red weeds, kelps and saw wrack near low water. Thin, shiny, almost transparent, and yellow with red bands, it has a chink on one side of the opening. It lays green rings of eggs in spring.

MOLLUSCS Gastropods: **needle and spire shells**
The spire shells, although tiny (about 6 mm high),
are very plentiful in mud, and are much eaten by
ducks and waders. **Laver spire shell** *Hydrobia ulvae*
1 is found in the intertidal mud of estuaries and
saltmarshes, where it feeds mainly on *Ulva* and
Enteromorpha but also on plankton. The brown,
elongated shell has 6 shallow whorls and a blunt tip.
It tolerates salinity from 33‰ (normal seawater)
down to 10‰, whereas *H. ventrosa* **2** occurs in mud
and on weed in brackish water from 20‰ down to
6‰ salinity. It has 6 or 7 plump, deeply defined
whorls and a pointed tip; does not occur in the north.
Jenkin's spire shell *Potamopyrgus jenkinsi* **3** is glossy,
yellowish and more solid, and has a large body whorl
two-thirds of the shell height. Sometimes the whorls
are keeled. It tolerates salinity below 15‰ is found
high up estuaries and is increasingly common in
rivers.

Bittium reticulatum **4** is aptly called the **needle
shell**, as its narrow, pointed spire of 15 whorls or so
may be 1.5 cm high but only 3 mm wide. It is rusty
brown with tiny, evenly-spaced knobs, often worn
white in washed-up specimens. **Common wendle-
trap** *Clathrus clathrus* **5** is a magnificent fawn shell,
up to 4 cm, with 15 deeply-defined whorls and
distinct ridges running across them like a spiral
staircase. It releases a purple dye if disturbed. Both
species, though mainly sublittoral, may be found
under stones among rocks at extreme low water, the
needle shell mainly in the west.

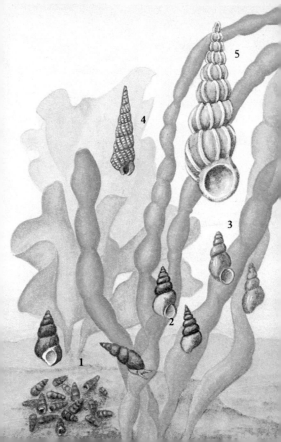

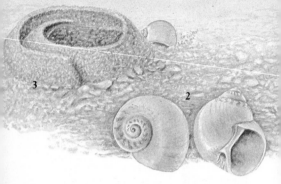

Molluscs Gastropods: **cowries, shells cast ashore**
Cowries have a unique form: the spire is absent from
the shell, and the oval body whorl has 20 or so ridges
and a narrow slit aperture running the full length of
the shell. In life the mantle covers the shell (**1a**). The
spotted or **European cowrie** *Trivia monacha* **1** is
about 1 cm long and pinkish, with 3 brown spots on
top of the shell, which is paler below. The white
cowrie *T. arctica* has no spots. The spotted cowrie
may be found under ledges at low water, feeding on
sea squirts.

The **common necklace shell** *Natica alderi* **2** burrows deep in sand at extreme low water and below,
where it preys on bivalves such as *Venus* (p. 132). Its
large, mobile foot, which in life can partially cover
the outside of the shell, expands by engorgement
with blood and seawater to hold the prey, whilst acid
from the proboscis tip dissolves a hole in the umbo

region of the bivalve. Through this, the flesh is scraped away by the radula. A long inhalant siphon draws water to the gills. Empty shells are often washed up—shiny, globular, mottled pale brown and to 2 cm across—as are the flat, curved 'choker necklace' egg masses, mixed with sand grains **3**.

The other two shells, though living in sublittoral sand and muddy gravel, are not infrequently cast ashore. The **pelican's foot shell** *Aporrhais pespelecani* **4**, to 6 cm, has beaded whorls, and the adults grow a flange drawn out into 'toes'. The **tower shell** *Turritella communis* **5**, to 5 cm, is tall and narrow, with many 3-ridged whorls and a small opening.

1

MOLLUSCS Gastropods: **whelks**

All whelks have tall, sturdy shells, with the mouth drawn out into a groove which accommodates a respiratory siphon, held aloft, above stirred-up mud to collect clear water. They are predators and at the end of a long proboscis have a radula with which they drill into prey shells. The creamy or greeny-grey **common dog whelk** *Nucella lapillus* **1** is very common on rocks and in crevices midshore, where it feeds on barnacles, mussels and topshells. The strong shell (to 4 cm) is variable: more ridged and pointed in sheltered conditions, but with a larger opening, which improves its grip on the rocks, in exposed places, and sometimes dark-banded, after a mussel diet. It can release a poisonous purple dye, purpurin. The ♀ attaches vase-shaped egg capsules, each containing hundreds of eggs, to crevices in early spring, and 4 months later a few miniature shells (1-2 mm) emerge, having eaten the remaining eggs. Juveniles feed on *Spirorbis* (p. 94).

The **sting winkle** or **drill** *Ocenebra erinacea* **2**, to 5 cm, has a more pointed, solid and sculptured shell, pale yellow with brown markings. Older shells may

118

have the siphon groove closed into a tube. It occurs on gravelly mud near rocks at ELWS and below, but moves upshore in summer to deposit egg capsules. Although mostly sublittoral, the large beige shell of the **common whelk** or **buckie** *Buccinum undatum* **3** and its egg mass (p. 230) are often washed up. Up to 10 cm tall, it is often encrusted with barnacles or inhabited by a hermit crab. The **netted dog whelk** *Nassarius reticulatus* **4** is brown, with a network pattern of squares, a thick-walled opening, toothed on its outer edge, and is 3-4 cm tall; the **thick-lipped dog whelk** *N. incrassatus* **5** is half the size. Both are common scavengers on sand and mud in stony places, can be collected using bait and used for keeping aquaria free of debris.

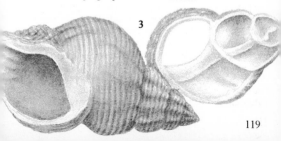

Molluscs Gastropods: **sea-slugs**

Sea-slugs are delicately beautiful and best viewed under water. Most live offshore and come ashore in spring and summer to spawn. Though molluscs, they have no protective shell, and many are camouflaged and secrete distasteful chemicals to deter predators.

The **sea hare** *Aplysia punctata* **1** comes ashore in spring to spawn strings of peach-coloured eggs on weed. It is common in some years, in pools and under weed, on which it feeds, in the kelp zone. It can reach 15 cm with no external gills and an internal shell, and may be red, brown or olive, often yellow-spotted, depending on diet and age. The foot is extended into two lateral flaps for swimming, and there are 4 tentacles, the forward ones broad, the hind standing up like ears. It ejects a purple slime when disturbed. The others here have external gills and no shell. The **common grey sea-slug** *Aeolidia papillosa* **2** is the largest (to 9 cm) shore sea-slug, often found beneath stones, and looking when retracted like the snakelocks anemone (p. 78) on which it feeds. It has 2 pairs of tentacles and many greyish cerata, giving it a furry look, with a parting down its back. Cerata contain gut branches and store defensive sting cells from the anemones it eats. In spring it spawns spiral gelatinous egg ribbons. *Facelina auriculata* **3** is pale and thin, to 2.5 cm long, with yellow, ridged posterior tentacles, and has 4-6 clusters of crimson, blue-tipped cerata; especially in the south and west. Widely distributed and found feeding on hydroids is the pale *Doto coronata* **4**, 1.2 cm, with crimson spots and 5-7 pairs of cerata in 2 rows down its back.

120

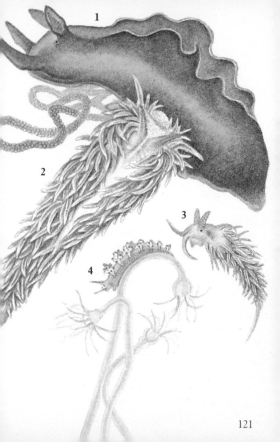

MOLLUSCS Gastropods: **Sea-slugs**

The commonest shore sea-slug is the **sea lemon** *Archidoris pseudoargus* **1**, which winters at sea, but may be found from spring onwards near its food, the breadcrumb sponge (p. 72), on which its warty yellow skin is well camouflaged. It is 7.5 cm long, with 2 tentacles and a ring of 9 retractable plumed gills round the anus. When these are retracted, it looks like a shell-less limpet, a dark area marking the site of the gills. It lays gleaming white egg ribbons, 2 cm wide, on weed in April, and then dies soon after.

The other sea-slugs here cannot retract their gills. *Goniodoris nodosa* **2** has a smooth, keeled, pale pink body, with paler specks, is 2.5 cm long, and has yellow

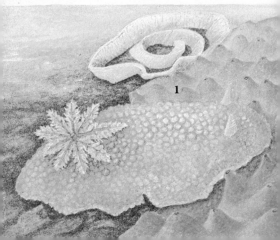

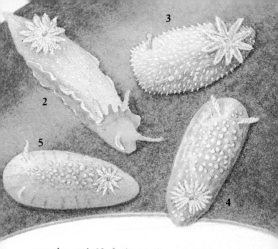

tentacles and 13 feathery gills around the anus. It breeds in March, feeds on seamats (p. 170) and sea squirts (p. 184-7), and is fairly common amongst rocks at low water. *Acanthodoris pilosa* **3** also feeds on seamats; it has 9 pinnate gills on its domed, white to greyish-purple body (1.5 cm), and long backward-pointing tentacles. At times *Onchidoris bilamellata* (*fusca*) **4** may be quite common on stones and piles at low water near the barnacles it feeds on. It has a pale body, 2.5 cm long, with tubercles and brown mottling, and 20 or more feathery gills incompletely circling the anus. *O. muricata* **5** is a smaller species, yellow with rusty spots and 10 gills. It feeds on sea-mats.

123

Molluscs Bivalves: **borers**

These bivalves bore into rock by the grinding action of their shells. As they grow, the bore of the tube widens and they become entombed; contact with the outside, essential for filter feeding, is made by their long siphons. *Hiatella arctica* **1**, the commonest rock borer, drills holes in pebbles and soft rocks, even wood, but is often found in crevices or in algal holdfasts, secured by byssus threads. Its thick, white, gaping oblong shell, 3-4 cm long, has a spiny ridge running across each valve, which becomes worn by the twisting of the shell against the rock. The red siphons are protected in a horny sheath and, when contracted, suddenly squirt water out of the tube. The brittle, delicate shell of the **common piddock** *Pholas dactylus* **2** is surprisingly strong, boring into slate, chalk and hard clays at low water and below in the south-west. Anchored by its foot to the end of the tube, the loose, gaping valves are rocked to and fro by alternate contraction of the two adductor muscles, the teeth, ridges and spines on the shell increasing the abrasion. The shell, about 12 cm long is sometimes washed up; holes about 1.5 cm across. Much damage is done to boats, piles and other wood by the **shipworm** *Teredo norvegica* **3**, whose chalky-lined, cylindrical tubes, up to 30 cm long, can riddle wood. Anchored by a tiny foot, the saw-toothed edge of the unhinged shell (1.7 cm) wears the wood away. The worm-like body extends the whole length of the tube, but only the front is covered by the shell. Two limy plates at the end of the separate siphons can close the tube. Shipworms also actually digest wood.

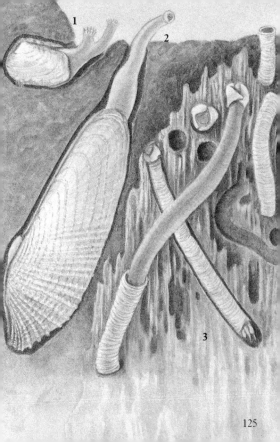

1

MOLLUSCS Bivalves: **mussels**

Mussels live on the surface of rocks, attached securely yet flexibly against waves by dark byssus threads, rather like guy-ropes, secreted by the foot. A thick horny layer, the periostracum, covers the shell.

The **edible mussel** *Mytilus edulis* **1** is abundant from the MTL down on piles, harbour walls, stones —any firm substrate. They compete with barnacles on rocks on exposed shores, yet there are vast beds on stones in estuaries. The largest mussels (to 10 cm) are near low water. The blue-black shell has a whitish or violet, pearly lining. They are filter feeders; 45 litres of water may pass in 24 hours through the frilly-edged inhalant opening. Mussels are harvested commercially, at about 3 years old. The **horse mussel** *Modiolus modiolus* **2** is larger, 5-15 cm, with the umbo above the narrow end of the shell (**2a**), not at the tip as in *Mytilus* (**1a**). It has a smooth mantle and brown shell; in

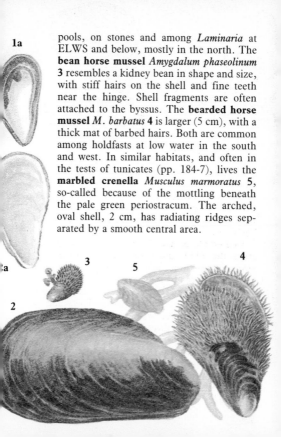

1a

pools, on stones and among *Laminaria* at ELWS and below, mostly in the north. The **bean horse mussel** *Amygdalum phaseolinum* **3** resembles a kidney bean in shape and size, with stiff hairs on the shell and fine teeth near the hinge. Shell fragments are often attached to the byssus. The **bearded horse mussel** *M. barbatus* **4** is larger (5 cm), with a thick mat of barbed hairs. Both are common among holdfasts at low water in the south and west. In similar habitats, and often in the tests of tunicates (pp. 184-7), lives the **marbled crenella** *Musculus marmoratus* **5**, so-called because of the mottling beneath the pale green periostracum. The arched, oval shell, 2 cm, has radiating ridges separated by a smooth central area.

Molluscs Bivalves **oysters and scallops**

All the shells on this plate live on the surface and hold their valves slightly apart to filter-feed. The **common saddle oyster** *Anomia ephippium* **1** is frequent from midshore down, very firmly attached to other shells, stones, and weeds by calcified byssus threads arising from a hole in the lower valve. The thin, white, pearl-lined valves are unequal, the upper being more convex, overgrowing the lower, and often taking on the contours of the substrate. The **European** or **native oyster** *Ostrea edulis* **2** is gregarious, cemented by the more convex lower valve to stones in shallow estuarine water, mostly in the south and south-east. The circular shells, smooth and white when young, but becoming grey and scaly in adults (8-15 cm), are often cast up, and bear a large central muscle scar. Living shells rarely contain a tiny pearl. The larvae are used to seed oyster beds.

Scallops are handsome bivalves and, though sublittoral, are often cast up. Attached when young by byssus threads which emerge from one of the 'ears', most are free swimmers as adults. They can achieve 'jet propulsion' for about 30 cm by rapidly closing the valves, which forces water out. A row of eyes and several of tentacles surround the mantle, providing warning of starfish, the main predator. The edible **great scallop** or **clam** *Pecten maximus* **3**, 10-15 cm across, has reddish or brown valves with 15-17 ribs, one more convex. The graded colours of the beautiful **queen scallop** *Aequipecten opercularis* **4**, 9 cm, are very varied. A good swimmer, with one valve flatter than the other and 18-22 rough ribs, it can also be eaten.

MOLLUSCS Bivalves: **cockles and trough shells**
The bivalves here are shallow burrowers, extending a short siphon to the surface, and anchoring themselves by protruding their foot. All but the common cockle live offshore, but the shells are often found on the strandline. The **dog cockle** *Glycymeris glycymeris* **1** has a thick circular shell, up to 5 cm diameter, pale with wavy brown patterning, and brown inside. Its semicircular hinge is toothed.

True cockles have thick, ribbed shells with a wavy margin, a prominent umbo, and are heart-shaped when the complete animal is viewed from the side. The **common cockle** *Cerastoderma edule* **2** is abundant (up to 1,000 per m^2) just below the surface in intertidal sandy mud in estuaries. They can be collected, allowed to filter for some hours to remove grittiness, then eaten. The shell, to 5 cm, has 22-28 flat, radiating ribs, which may be slightly spiny, and concentric markings. The **prickly cockle** *Acanthocardia echinata* **3**, however, is larger (7 cm), with 19-21 ribs, armed with spines connected at their base. The **little cockle** *Parvicardium exiguum* **4** has a smaller, darker shell, 1.5 cm, with 25 ribs bearing tubercles when young.

The trough shells are thinner, smoother and triangular, with fine concentric grooves. the **rayed trough** *Mactra corallina* **5** is large (to 5 cm), with light brown rays on a cream ground, and purplish inside. The **cut trough** *Spisula subtruncata* **6** is smaller (2.5 cm), lacks the rays, and is also common, especially on the east coast.

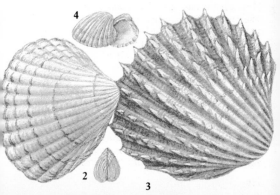

4

2

3

MOLLUSCS Bivalves: *Venus and carpet shells*
These are burrowing shells, in clean sand around low
water and below. All have concentric growth lines, the
beak facing towards the front of the shell, which has 2
muscle scars and a loop in the mantle scar—the sinus.
Venus shells are triangular in outline, with a serrated
inside edge. The **warty venus** *Venus verrucosa* **1** is the
largest (6 cm), solid, arched and pale brown, with strong
concentric ridges, warty at one side; south and west
only. Pale valves to 4.5 cm with overlapping ridges and 3
rusty rays are very common and belong to the **striped
venus** *Chamelea (Venus) striatula* **2** which burrows in
sandy gravel from low water down to around 100 m.
The **banded venus** *Clausinella (Venus) fasciata* **3** is a
smaller (2.5 cm), sturdier shell, with 10 distinct ridges
like steps, and may be white, yellow, red or brown, sometimes with darker rays. Though sublittoral, it can be found
occasionally under stones on gravel. The **pullet carpet
shell** *Venerupis pullastra* **4** and the **banded carpet** *V.
rhomboides* **5** are oval shells with a smooth inside edge,
the beak towards the front and the other end wedge-
shaped. The pullet carpet (5 cm) occurs just below the
surface of muddy gravel on the lower shore, attached by
byssus threads. It is reddish-brown, with fine radiating
ribs. The banded carpet, to 6 cm, is sublittoral, glossy
with flatter ridges, purplish marks and a more rounded
rear edge. The **rayed artemis** *Dosinia exoleta* **6**, 6 cm,
burrows deep in muddy gravel offshore, but its almost
round white valves, with shallow concentric ridges and
smooth inside edges, are often cast up. It has a large
sinus scar and distinct depression in front of the hinge.

Molluscs Bivalves: **wedge shell and tellins**

The bivalves here, unlike those on other plates, feed on detritus; they have a large foot and very compressed shells for burrowing, and divided siphons. The **banded wedge shell** *Donax vittatus* 1 is common from midshore down, mainly on exposed sandy shores. The valves, to 3 by 1.5 cm and with one end more pointed, are glossy and have fine radiating striations and concentric shading in bright purple, brown or yellow. The white or mauve interior has a fine-toothed edge. The **Faroe sunset shell** *Gari fervensis* 2, to 5 cm, though sublittoral, is often washed up. It has a blunt, gaping, keeled posterior end, pinkish rays, and a dark edge of periostracum. The inside is mauve and glossy. The tellins below are deep burrowers with very flattened shells, which ease movement through sand, and a longer inhalant siphon than exhalant. The fragile, very flat **thin tellin** *Tellina tenuis* 3 has shiny, pinkish valves to 2 cm, which are often found spread like butterfly wings, attached by the strong ligament. It is very common from the MTL down, 12 cm deep in clean sand. The **blunt tellin** *Arcopagia* (*Tellina*) *crassa* 4 is larger (to 5 cm) and more solid, with distinct concentric ridges on its cream shell. Common in coarse sand beyond low water. The **Baltic tellin** *Macoma*

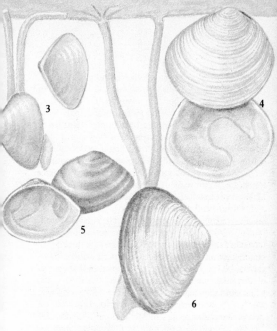

balthica **5** has a thick, oval, more convex shell (2.5 cm), with concentric bands of white and pink. The **peppery furrow shell** *Scrobicularia plana* **6**, 5 cm, burrows to 20 cm in brackish estuaries, leaving a star-like impression on the mud, where its siphon has been drawing up material. The flat, oval, pale valves have concentric furrows.

MOLLUSCS Bivalves: **razor shells and gapers**
When alive, razor shells burrow vertically in clean sand near low water. They are filter feeders with short, fused siphons and a very long, mobile foot, which they use for burrowing and anchorage. Razors are sensitive to vibrations and can move down (and up) in the sand extremely rapidly, sending a jet of water out of the siphons as they do. The **pod razor** or **spout-fish** *Ensis siliqua* **1** is collected for bait; it has a rectangular shell, to 20 cm, while the smaller **sword razor** *E. ensis* **2** has a curved shell, 10 cm long, tapering at one end.

The other shells here lie deeply buried and delve deeper (to 40 cm) as they grow. They have a smaller foot, but the immensely long, retractable fused siphons make contact with the surface, for these too are filter feeders; they appear as a tentacle-fringed figure-of-8 in the sand. Their large, flattened oval shells gape in life; the valves are washed up, especially in winter. The **sand gaper** *Mya arenaria* **3**, the edible clam eaten in the US, is very common in estuaries. It is brownish, 12 cm long, and being much less mobile than the razor shells, cannot reburrow if dug up. The **blunt gaper** *M. truncata* **4**, to 8 cm, is more solid, with concentric grooves and one rectangular end. Common in muddy gravel and sand at low water and below, as is the **common otter shell** *Lutraria lutraria* **5**, whose glossy cream, oblong shell has a brown periostracum and reaches 15 cm. The hinge teeth differ from those on gapers.

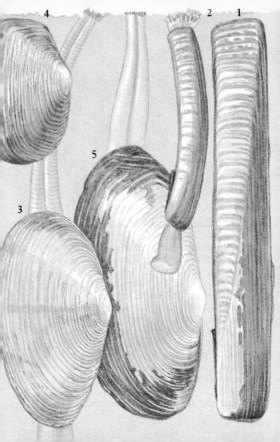

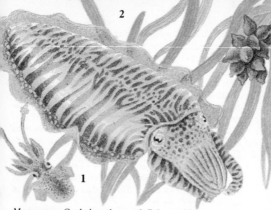

Molluscs Cephalopods: **cuttlefish, squid and octopus**

Cuttlefish have an internal cuttlebone (pp. 230-231) or air-filled buoyancy organ and, like other cephalopods, release a cloud of brown ink (sepia) from the anus to escape predators such as fish, eels and seals. They have 8 tentacles with suckers round the beak-like jaws, and 2 longer ones with suckers only on their broad tips. The **little cuttlefish** *Sepiola atlantica* **1**, to 5 cm, is not uncommonly found on or buried in sand in shallow water, where it feeds on shrimps. It is round, often luminescent and has diamond-shaped fins. The **common cuttlefish** *Sepia officinalis* **2** has a broad body, to 30 cm, and moves gently back and forth over the sand by undulating its complete fringe of fins, often amongst *Zostera*. It uncovers shrimps and crabs by gently disturbing the sand with water expelled from its funnel. Cuttlefish are masters of disguise and can change colour rapidly and may be disruptively striped. They are occasional, found mainly in summer and in the south. The **common squid** *Loligo forbesi* **3** comes into shallower water to spawn and may be washed up, especially on the east coast. It is greyish, up to 60 cm, and has triangular fins and 10 tentacles. Sometimes the internal shell (the 'pen') is cast up. Octopuses have 8 equal, webbed tentacles, a bag-like body, and although they can swim, tend to lurk in rock cavities or occasionally in pools at ELWS. The **curled octopus** *Eledone cirrhosa* **4**, (to 50 cm), is mainly northern; it has a single row of suckers on each arm, while the **common octopus** *Octopus vulgaris* is restricted to the south coast and has double rows of suckers on each tentacle.

Arthropods

This phylum has a vast number of species to be found in almost all habitats and with diverse adaptations. All, however, have a horny outside skeleton, the **exoskeleton**, jointed body and legs, and irregular growth by moulting (often involving distinct larval and adult forms) due to the constraints imposed by the external skeleton. Of the major groups, only the crustacea have mastered marine life. They are abundant on the seashore, and in the plankton; copepods such as *Calanus* are an essential part of food chains.

Crustacea have 2 pairs of **antennae** and 5 or more pairs of legs (c.f. insects with 1 pair of antennae and 3 pairs of legs; spiders with no antennae and 4 pairs of legs). The head, with various jaw appendages, is often fused to the thorax which may be covered by a **carapace**. Unlike insects they have gills which must remain moist to absorb oxygen. Most crustacea move freely but adult barnacles are firmly cemented to the rock, and were once thought to be molluscs. The planktonic larvae, attracted by chemicals, settle on rocks already inhabited by barnacles, in densities as high as 100,000 per m^2. Barnacles are hermaphrodite, and mate by protruding the penis into a neighbouring barnacle. From the **operculum** (the 2 moveable plates) 6 pairs of feathery thoracic legs, the **cirri**, emerge, moving to and fro collecting food and oxygen.

The basic plan of all crustaceans is to have 8 thoracic and 6 abdominal segments all with limbs variously modified, but in many cases segments are fused and appendages reduced or lost.

Opossum shrimps are transparent little 'shrimps'

which dart about in pools. They have many legs, a thin carapace and no pincers. Sea slaters hide away in damp cracks in daylight, and emerge in large numbers to scavenge at night. Like woodlice they can curl up; the last pair of appendages, the **uropods**, form a 'tail'. Slaters and sandhoppers have 7 pairs of thoracic legs and no carapace. Whilst in slaters all the legs are similar, those of sandhoppers are modified for walking, swimming and jumping. Sandhoppers have flattened bodies, and the tail is curled under giving spring. Some swim on their sides. Huge numbers are eaten by waders.

Prawns, shrimps, lobsters and crabs are decapods, all with 5 pairs of walking or swimming legs, some with pincers and a hardened carapace. Prawns, essentially pool-dwellers, differ from the sand-living shrimps in being flattened laterally and in having a projecting **rostrum**. They have a remarkable ability to change colour. Crabs have their reduced abdomen tucked underneath; this is most easily seen in primitive forms like hermit crabs. They walk sideways and beating plates on the jaw which draw water over the gills can clearly be seen.

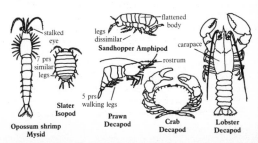

stalked eye

7 prs similar legs

Slater Isopod

Opossum shrimp Mysid

flattened body

legs dissimilar

Sandhopper Amphipod

carapace

rostrum

5 prs walking legs

Prawn Decapod

Crab Decapod

Lobster Decapod

CRUSTACEANS Cirripedes: **barnacles**

Barnacles vary in shape and size, taller when crowded, flatter on exposed shores. The **star** *Chthamalus stellatus* **1**, to 1.2 cm across, is very common in the south-west and west on the upper part of exposed shores. In more sheltered areas they extend less far down the shore due to competition from *Balanus balanoides*. Both terminal plates are overlapped by the laterals, the operculum is kite-shaped and has the sutures crossing at right-angles. The **acorn barnacle** *B. balanoides* **2**, to 1.5 cm, has only one terminal plate overlapped and the other appears wider as it overlaps its neighbours. The suture pattern on the diamond-shaped operculum is quite different from *C. stellatus*. It is abundant and commonest in the north, but always below *C. stellatus* where they both occur, favouring MHWN to MLWN on less exposed shores. *B. perforatus* **3**, the largest barnacle (to 3 cm) has smooth pale purplish plates, often jagged round the top edge, and an off-centre opening. It is found below *B. balanoides*, in the south-west only, while *B. crenatus* (to 1.2 cm) occurs lowest of all, on all coasts, on shells, crabs and stones, but rarely exposed. Its pale grey, ridged shell is lop-sided, and the opercular plates have a yellow rim. The **Darwin barnacle** *Elminius modestus* **5**, (1 cm), was introduced from Australia about 40 years ago and is spreading northwards. Found high on not too exposed upper middle shores, often near freshwater seepage, it has 4 (not 6) grey plates, as has the tiny white warty barnacle, *Verruca stroemia* **6**, 6 mm, found singly very low on the shore, often on kelp roots. It has unequal, longitudinally ribbed plates, an asymmetrical operculum, and a neat base outline.

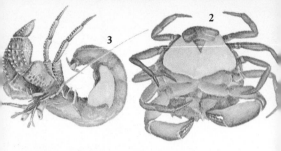

CRUSTACEANS Cirripedes: **barnacles**

Although really pelagic, the **goose barnacle** *Lepas anatifera* **1** is not infrequently found attached to driftwood or even bottles or boat hulls, when it can slow down the boat considerably. It consists of a leathery, wrinkled greyish-brown stalk, 10-20 cm long, which is attached to a flattened shell, 5 cm across, made of 5 thin, whitish-grey plates, from which feathery tentacles (known as cirri) extrude to trap food. The name derives from the resemblance to the head and neck of a goose. It was once thought they gave rise to migratory geese, and the barnacle goose, a small black and white goose which winters on British shores, gets its name from this belief. Another species, *L. fascicularis*, secretes its own float, to which several barnacles attach.

The next two barnacles are parasitic and are so modified, with loss of shell, appendages and gut, that it is only the larval stages that show their affinities. The **parasitic barnacle** *Sacculina carcini* **2** forms a smooth, pale yellow growth, 2 by 1.2 cm, on the underside of its host, the shore crab *Carcinus maenas* (p. 160). It is very common and prevents the crab from fully tucking its tail under. Although it grows where the female carries her eggs, it is not granular like those, and infests both sexes, causing male crabs to show female characteristics and females to appear immature. Branches from the sac penetrate the host tissue, absorbing food. *Peltogaster paguri* **3** is a parasite of the hermit crab *Pagurus bernhardus* (p. 159). Its smooth, curved, yellow or red sac, about 1.2 cm across, is a common feature under the crab's tail, but can only be seen if the crab is removed from its shell.

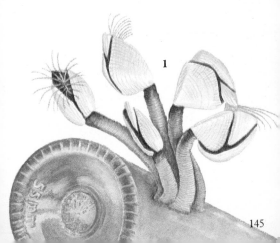

CRUSTACEANS Leptostraca and Mysids: **opossum shrimps**

The shade-loving, shrimp-like *Nebalia bipes* 1, 1 cm long, often occurs in large numbers under stones or amongst rotting weed on the lower shore. It is orange or greenish-yellow, with prominent red, stalked eyes and a rostral spine projecting between them. The lower pair of antennae is longer than the upper—as long as the body on the male. A thin, loose shell, divided at the mid-back, covers all the thoracic and 4 pairs of abdominal legs. The remaining species here are opossum shrimps (mysids), so-called because the females carry the eggs and young in ventral brood-pouches. They are dainty, often transparent, hanging vertically in the water among *Zostera* in pools or at the edge of the sea, and in brackish water, at the heads of lochs or estuaries. They swim rapidly with flicks of the tail. They have prominent black eyes on long stalks, 8 thoracic

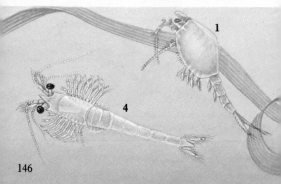

legs with bristles but no pincers, short swimmerets on the abdomen and a broad tail fan. The 1st pair of thoracic legs creates a current which flows under the carapace, aerating the animal and bringing plankton which is filtered by the hairy mouthparts. Larger morsels can be bitten by the jaws. The commonest is the **chamaeleon shrimp** *Praunus flexuosus* **2**, 1.8-2.5 cm, whose curved body blends accurately with its background—green, grey and black. The carapace does not quite cover the last thoracic segment and it has a cleft in the spine-edged tail segment. The **ghost shrimp** *Schistomysis spiritus* **3**, 1.8 cm, is also abundant. It is transparent except for its black eyes, and the tail segments have wavy edges, a wide cleft and spines. *Siriella armata* **4** is slender, 2 cm long, and almost transparent except for a rusty coloration towards the spiny, uncleft tail. The outer parts of the uropods are jointed near the tip. Common in pools.

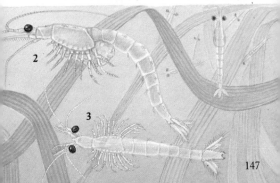

CRUSTACEANS Isopods: **sea slaters**

The ash-coloured *Jaera albifrons* **1**, ♀ 4 mm, ♂ 3 mm, is common under stones below MTL, often in estuaries. Its outer antennae are ½ the length of the oval body, the wide head has a whitish forehead and large eyes, and there are deep hair-fringed notches between the segments, especially between thorax and abdomen. Short uropods just project beyond a notch on the wide tail plate. The following common species have the uropods divided into two broad fins which, with the tail segment, form a fan. *Eurydice pulchra* **2** (♂ 8 mm, ♀ slightly smaller) is a carnivore in wet sand or actively swimming in pools below MTL. Its elliptical body has a domed upper surface, rather transparent and pale grey, with darker starry markings, and its outer antennae are ½ body length. The front 3 pairs of legs are short and hooked, and the last 4 long and hairy. The hairy uropods extend just beyond the rounded tail segment. Submerged wood is often riddled with holes 5 mm wide, made by the **gribble** *Limnoria lignorum* **3**. This brown crustacean, 2 x 5 mm, has short antennae, short spiny uropods just longer than the tail segment, and can roll its body, with its long thorax and parallel-sided abdomen, into a ball when disturbed. *Gnathia maxillaris* **4** is green, blue or grey, with short antennae, 5 pairs of thoracic legs, and a pointed abdomen, much narrower than the thorax; in water under stones and weed around LW. Males (6 mm) have prominent hooked mandibles and are widest across the head. Females are slightly longer, lack jaws, may be spotted and egg-bearing, and are widest across the thorax.

148

CRUSTACEANS Isopods: **sea slaters**

Abundant under stones midshore, in estuaries and in saltmarsh pools is *Sphaeroma rugicauda* **1**, whose domed body is oval and half as wide as long ($\male$ 1 cm, $\female$ smaller). It has outer antennae ⅓ body length and a rough tail segment, flanked by large, flattened, split uropods. Greyish, with darker markings and a light mid-dorsal strip, *Sphaeroma* swims on its back and curls up if disturbed. The **sea slater** *Ligia oceanica* **2** is a large (2.8 cm $\male$, 2 cm $\female$), fast-running isopod inhabiting damp cracks and crevices, and under stones above high water mark. Semi-terrestrial, it cannot tolerate long immersion but at night large numbers emerge to browse the brown algae. The body is oval and flattened, with large black eyes, stout outer antennae ⅔ body length, a greenish-grey rough back with paler markings, and several exposed abdominal segments. Males have 7 pairs of legs, females 6, and the uropods are long, trailing and forked. Seven species of *Idotea* inhabit the lower part of the shore. Nocturnal, gregarious scavengers, particularly on seaweed, they all have oblong bodies with slightly convex sides and a tail plate (formed from fused abdominal segments) with no uropods visible from above. All have outer antennae about ⅓ body length. *I. neglecta* **3**, dark brown or black with paler markings and very common, has a keeled, bluntly rounded tail plate, and slender long antennae. The narrow, reddish-brown or greenish body of *I. granulosa* **4** has a pitted surface; the end plate has no keel and narrows to a sharp point. *I. emarginata* **5** is the largest (♂ to 3 cm), dark brown and sometimes spotted, with a rounded tail plate ending in a concave notch; common amongst weed.

CRUSTACEANS Amphipods: **sand-hoppers, sand shrimps and skeleton shrimps**

Talitrus saltator **1** and *Orchestia gammarella* **2** are common sandhoppers of the upper shore which can jump 20 cm or more when disturbed, by flicking their curved tails. *Talitrus* is tank-like, 1.6 cm long, with a black line down its back, and upper antennae shorter than the lower; 2nd walking leg is curved and claw-like. At night it emerges from burrows to scavenge amongst rotting weed along the strand-line. *Orchestia* may extend slightly further down the shore amongst weed and stones. It is larger (to 2 cm), with a huge claw on the 3rd walking leg. Under stones on the lower shore the **sand shrimp** *Gammarus locusta* **3** is very common. If disturbed, it wriggles on its side, often clasped in pairs. Its curved olivey body ($\female$ 1.4 cm, $\male$ 2 cm) has branched upper antennae (only visible under water), shorter lower ones and 7 thoracic legs which get progressively longer. There are several species, each restricted to different salinity ranges. The similar *Amphithoë rubricata* **4**, to 1.2 cm, is found amongst weed, and under stones on coarse sandy shores at all levels. It has small red eyes, heavier nippers and unbranched upper antennae. *Corophium volutator* **5** occurs in vast numbers (up to 10,000/m^2) in midshore burrows in estuarine or saltmarsh mud. Its buff body is not flattened, has heavy lower antennae twice body length, and the 7th pair of walking legs is much the longest. The wiry skeleton shrimp *Caprella linearis* **6**, $\female$ 1.4 cm and $\male$ 2 cm, rests motionless on hydroids and weeds and seizes plankton. Upper antennae are twice the length of the hairy lower ones; the $\female$ carries eggs in her brood-pouch.

152

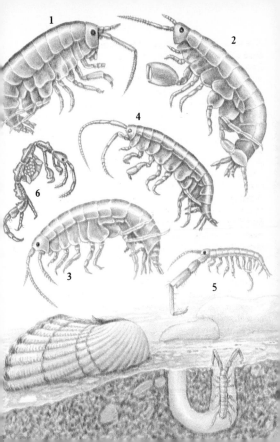

CRUSTACEANS Decapods: **prawns and shrimps**
The shape and serration of the rostrum (p. 140-1) are critical for the identification of prawns.

The **common prawn** *Palaemon serratus* **1**, to 10 cm, is greyish with purplish markings. The outer antennae may be 1½ times body length, and the 2nd pair of legs is the longest, with fine feeding pincers. It can move rapidly backwards if disturbed. Commonest in the south and west, in deep pools or at low water, *P. serratus* is edible—it turns pink on boiling. *P. elegans* (*squilla*) **2** is similar (to 5 cm) and also edible; it is found from April to September, especially in the east.

Another edible prawn is the **Aesop prawn** *Pandalus montagui* **3**, 5-7 cm, semi-transparent with red markings and red-striped antennae. One of the 2nd pair of walking legs is noticeably longer than the other; found in rock pools, brackish water and sublittorally.

The **chamaeleon prawn** *Hippolyte varians* **4**, 2 cm, blends well with the background, being green, reddish, brown, or clear blue at night. Its outer antennae are ½ as long as the humped body. It is common in estuaries and saltmarshes, as is the **edible shrimp** *Crangon crangon* **5**, to 5 cm, which lies buried by day, camouflaged in sand on the lower shore, with only antennae tips protruding. Flatter than prawns, greyish in colour with red mottling, there is no rostrum; the antennae are almost body length, and the 1st pair of legs have large pincers, the 2nd small ones.

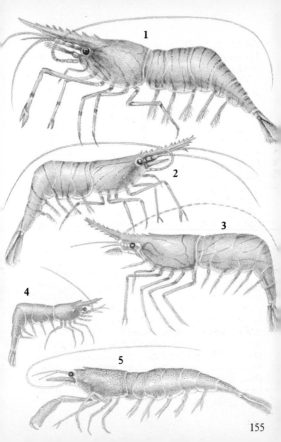

CRUSTACEANS Decapods: **lobsters and
squat lobsters**

The **edible lobster** *Homarus gammarus* **1** is the largest
British crustacean (25-60 cm), and though usually
sublittoral on all coasts, it may lurk in deep rock
pools in summer. It is blue, brownish-blue or reddish with white spots, with long red antennae, but
turns bright red when boiled. The huge 1st pair of
walking legs has unequally-sized claws, the stronger
used for cracking, the weaker for grasping. It usually
crawls, but can swim backwards. The ♀ breeds once
every 2 years and carries the numerous developing
eggs underneath.

The **crawfish** or **spiny** or **rock lobster** *Palinurus
elephas* (*vulgaris*) **2**, 30-45 cm, differs from the true
lobster in lacking large pincers. However, the brown-

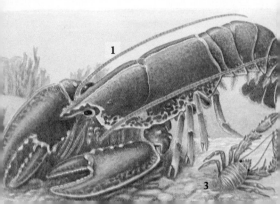

ish or purplish body is armed with pale spines and long flailing antennae, which can whip painfully. Found in the south-west only and usually sublittoral, but occasionally in clefts in pools, it is eaten in France as *langouste*.

The much smaller **squat lobster** *Galathea squamifera* **3**, to 5 cm, migrates inshore in the spring, when it is not infrequent under stones in lower shore pools on all coasts. The abdomen of this greenish-brown lobster is kept tucked under the body except when is using its tail as a paddle for rapid evasive backwards propulsion. It has a rostrum and the carapace has tubercles and transverse ridges; the first pair of legs is twice body length and spiny with heavy claws. It appears to have only 4 pairs of legs as the 5th pair is folded within the gill chamber.

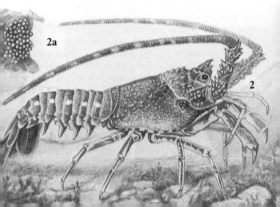

2a

2

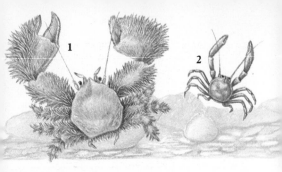

CRUSTACEANS Decapods: **crabs**

The porcelain crabs *Porcellana platycheles* **1**, the **broad-clawed** and *P. longicornis* **2**, the **long-clawed**, resemble squat lobsters in having the abdomen tucked under the thorax, very long antennae, and a greatly reduced 5th pair of legs folded beneath. *P. platycheles* has a round, greyish-brown carapace, slightly longer (1.2 cm) than broad, with a ragged, hairy edge, and is usually mud-coated. Its antennae are long, and the large, equal, flattened nippers on the 1st pair of legs (3 cm long) have hairs on their outer edges; the other legs are hairy. *P. longicornis* is similar but has a smaller carapace, 0.4 cm long, and is hairless and shiny browny-red. The 1st pair of legs are long (about 1 cm) and more slender, with unequal nippers. Both are very common clinging closely under stones and amongst holdfasts from midshore down, but *P. platycheles* favours muddy gravel, *P. longicornis* clearer water. The **common hermit crab** *Pagurus bernhardus* **3**, to 12 cm, is abundant in pools and sandy flats. Aggressive and active and great fun to observe, it has no carapace and protects its soft, curved abdomen in an empty snail shell, especially those of edible periwinkle (p. 112) and common whelk (p. 118), not tucked under the body as in other crabs. The opening of the shell can rapidly be blocked by the large, red or yellow right nipper. The crab transfers to larger shells as it grows—the adults are mostly sublittoral. Frequently *Nereis fucata*, a ragworm, is commensal in the shell and the anemone *Calliactis parasitica* and hydroid *Hydractinia* on the shell—an excellent site for food gathering.

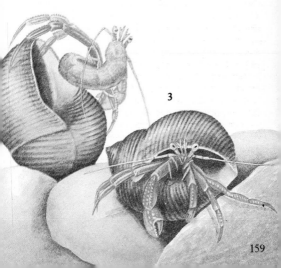

CRUSTACEANS Decapods: **crabs**

The **shore crab** *Carcinus maenas* **1** is the commonest crab on all shores and at all levels, even estuaries. It burrows in sand, hides under weed, in crevices, under stones and in pools. The knobbly dark blackish-green carapace is wider (to 10 cm) than long and often patterned with red or white in young animals. It has 3 teeth between the eyes and 5 sharp teeth either side behind the eyes. Females may be found with yellow eggs underneath; they have a wider 'purse' (the curved tail) underneath than males. Both sexes may be parasitised by the barnacle *Sacculina* (p. 144).

The **edible crab** *Cancer pagurus* **2** occurs low on the shore and below; young animals often occur among stones and weed, the larger firmly wedged in cracks. Its pinkish-brown carapace is oval, about 10 cm long by 15 cm wide, with 9 or so indentations either side like a pie-crust, and 3 small lobes between the eyes. The 1st pair of walking legs has huge black-tipped pincers; other legs are hairy.

One of the most handsome shore crabs is the **fiddler** or **velvet swimming crab** *Macropipus puber* **3**. Among rocks and weed very low on south and west coasts, sometimes thinly covered by sand, the fiddler waves its first legs, snapping its pincers fiercely if threatened. The carapace resembles *Carcinus* but is reddish-brown with soft hairs, and 8-10 teeth between the red eyes. The legs have blue lines and joints and the large 5th pair end not in spines, but in broad swimming paddles.

CRUSTACEANS Decapods: **crabs**

The **hairy crab** *Pilumnus hirtellus* **1** is indeed covered in hairs. The brownish-red carapace, wider (2.5 cm) than long (1.8 cm), has a notch between the eyes, and the large pale brown nippers are unequal; common in the south-west at low water under stones, amongst broken shells and in Laminarian holdfasts. A dainty green crab, speckled with purplish or red markings and found not infrequently on clean gravel low on the shore is *Pirimela denticulata* **2**; it is 1.2 cm long, slightly wider, with 3 teeth between the eyes and 7 down either side.

The **pea crab** *Pinnotheres pisum* **3** is a common commensal in mussels, cockles and oysters, where it filters food from the current drawn in by the host. The tiny round, soft-bodied crabs are yellowish; ♂ is 6 mm broad and ♀ 8 mm and more transparent; mainly found in the south and west.

The only truly burrowing crab is *Corystes cassivelaunus* **4** the **masked crab**, which, though really sublittoral, can be found in the south between April and July, especially in May. At other times carapaces of dead crabs may be washed up. The yellow-brown carapace has mask-like markings and is much longer (4 cm) than broad, and the first pair of legs is twice body length in the ♂, shorter in the ♀. Its long hairy antennae form a vent down which water can be drawn from the surface to the gills, as the crab buries itself in clean sand at ELWS. At night *Corystes* comes to the surface to scavenge and to mate.

CRUSTACEANS Decapods: **spider crabs**

These crabs, with their small bodies and long, slender, rather rigid legs, look very spider-like, and are often camouflaged by epiphytes, or even sponges and hydroids on the larger species, sometimes placed on the carapace by the crab. The **spiny spider crab** *Maia squinado* **1** has a pear-shaped, reddish-brown carapace, often blotched with pink or white, with 6 or so spines down each side. It is longer (18 cm) than broad and tapers in front to a split horned rostrum. Occurs among rocks and under weed at low water in the south-west, rare in the north.

Very much smaller and distinctly spidery is the **small spider crab** *Macropodia tenuirostris* **2**, which is common on all coasts, under stones and amongst weed near low water and below. Its triangular, yellow, green or dull brown carapace (1.7 cm long) has 8 spines and extends to form a long divided rostrum. The stalked eyes cannot be retracted. The 1st pair of legs bears pincers; legs 2-5 are extremely long, thin and hairy—indeed the 2nd pair are at least 3 times body length. The 2nd and 3rd pairs have straight, sharp tips, while the 4th and 5th end in an incurved hook. *Hyas araneus* **3** has a dull purple or brownish carapace, to 7 cm long, with no spines but with bristles and tubercles; found in deep pools among weeds, and in the Laminarian zone and below. The rostral horns converge and may touch and the eyes are retractable; does not occur in the north.

Insects and Pycnogonids: **sea spiders**
Although a highly successful class of arthropods on land and in air and freshwater, insects appear ill-adapted to marine life. Apart from strand-line flies, only 2 species are common, both on the upper shore and splash-zone.

The **bristletail** *Petrobius maritimus* **1** lives in cracks and crevices on upper shore rocks over which it can move rapidly, even jumping. Its body, 1 cm, has long antennae, 3 pairs of legs, no wings, and terminates in 3 bristles, the middle one being about body length. Floating on the surface film of small, still rock pools on the upper shore, clusters or rafts of tiny grey-blue springtails *Anurida littorale* **2** may often be seen. About 3 mm long, with 6 stubby legs and short antennae, it also crawls over rocks and shelters in cracks.

Sea spiders, Pycnogonida, like land spiders have 4 pairs of legs, but their abdomen is greatly reduced and there is a proboscis terminating in the mouth. *Pycnogonium littorale* **3** is a small, dull brown spider (1.5 cm) with short, chunky, clawed legs, and although common on lower rocky shores, is difficult to pick out as it clings to the column of the beadlet anemone *Actinia equina* (p. 78), on which it preys, or as it crawls on hydroids or under stones. The male carries the eggs on a special pair of legs near the mouth. *Nymphon* species are found in similar habitats but their legs are long and spindly: a related deep-sea species has a leg span of over half a metre.

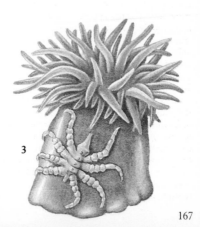

3

Seamats, echinoderms and tunicates

Seamats are abundant between the tides, where they either encrust weeds or take on a plant-like form themselves. They are colonial, each **zooid** secreting a calcareous or horny capsule into which it can withdraw its tentacles when exposed. Through a lens, the beauty and regularity of the colonial pattern is revealed. They are filter feeders, the hairs on the tentacles creating a current towards the mouth, where particles are sieved. Although some, such as *Bugula*, appear similar to hydroids (pp. 74-75), they have a more complex body-plan with an internal fluid-filled cavity; increased pressure on this causes eversion of the tentacles.

The echinoderms are of 5 types, which, though superficially dissimilar, all have a 5-fold symmetry, an internal skeleton of limy plates which carry tubercles or spines, and double rows of pliant, fluid-filled **tubefeet** in usually 5 grooves. Many have remarkable powers of regeneration. The feather star is a very primitive animal; its fossil relatives (crinoids) are common in palaeozoic rocks. Starfish detect their prey (mussels, scallops) using sensitive tubefeet on the end of their flexible arms, and move on the suckered tubefeet beneath them. The long slender arms of brittlestars are well delineated from the flat disc and they have a ventral mouth but no anus. They move by horizontal rippling of any 2 leading arms. The pointed tubefeet are coated with mucus and transport debris along the arms to the mouth. Sea urchins are rather inactive but use tubefeet for locomotion, have a **test** (internal shell) of fused plates, moveable spines and pincer-like **pedicellariae** on their body surface, for defence and removal of debris. All regular sea urchins, both browsers (e.g. *Echinus*) and carnivores (e.g. *Psammechinus*) have a complex mouthpart called **Aristotle's lantern**. Its intricacy can be seen on tests washed ashore. Burrowing heart urchins have an oval bilateral symmetry—mouth in front, anus behind—important for unidirectional movement, and lack the lantern, using tubefeet to collect particles in the sand. Sea cucumbers are aptly named: these slimy, bilaterally symmetrical animals lack spines and arms, but have tubefeet (though fewer) and small spicules embedded in the skin. A circle of tubefeet round the mouth collects detritus.

Adult sea-squirts appear simple and jelly-like, reminiscent of sponges, but in fact possess a **pharynx** suggestive of the gill chamber of fishes, where food can be filtered and oxygen absorbed. Indeed their larval stage is a 'tadpole' with a primitive 'backbone' (notochord), a feature possessed by all chordates including man, suggesting that in an evolutionary sense they are quite advanced.

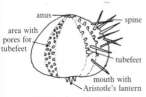

Side view of regular urchin with spines partially removed

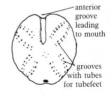

Dorsal view of irregular urchin test

Bryozoans: **seamats**

Seamats are colonies of tiny animals (zooids), which secrete a protective capsule from which ciliated tentacles extrude under water to collect plankton (see p. 168). *Membranipora membranacea* **1** is abundant on *Laminaria* and *Fucus* from midshore down; its whitish, oblong capsules are regularly arranged into a snakeskin pattern tracery. Colonies have an irregular outline, and a large one may be composed of several million individuals. Each capsule has a spine at 2 corners of one end, and a rigid base and sides, but a flexible 'membranous' lid, which, when pulled down, increases the fluid pressure in the zooid so that the tentacles are everted. *Flustrellidra* (*Flustrella*) *hispida* **2** forms a thick, greyish-brown, encrusting ring round the base of *Gigartina* (p. 48) especially, but also *Chondrus*, *Ascophyllum* and *Fucus*, and is very common. The oval capsules have a fringe of reddish spines along one side, and when in water the rather large zooids emerge, suggesting a bluish haze.

Under overhangs, among red weeds and sponges on the lower half of the shore, *Bugula turbinata* **3** is common. Superficially like a hanging tufted plant, it is yellow or orange, 3-5 cm, and its regularly divided branches are spirally arranged round the stem. *Alcyonidium gelatinosum* **4** looks like a dull green or yellow sponge. The capsules, which appear as raised dots, are embedded in jelly, and the lobed colony is either encrusting or upright; found low on shore, but the dried velvety colonies, 20 cm, are often cast up.

ECHINODERMS **feather star and starfish**

Though really sublittoral, the rosy **feather star** *Antedon bifida* **1**, to 10 cm diameter, may be found in sheltered crevices at extreme low water in the south-west only. Five pairs of reddish, feathery arms, often white-banded, arise from a small cup-shaped disc, and they attach temporarily to rocks by jointed bristles at the base of the cup. Their waving arms collect plankton and pass it to the upward-facing mouth, near which is the anus.

Starfish usually have 5 distinct arms, with 2 rows of tubefeet down the paler underside of each, a mouth in the centre of the lower surface, and anus on the upper. Most feed by everting the stomach over their prey, digesting and absorbing it, and leaving behind the waste. The **cushion star** *Asterina gibbosa* **2**, 2-10 cm, is quite common in the south and west near low water, on overhangs, under stones in pools, or nestling in holdfasts. It is stiff and rough, green or mauve with red markings, and has 5 very short stubby arms; it feeds on worms, bristlestars and small bivalves and lays eggs on stones. The **common sunstar** *Crossaster papposus* **3**, to 20 cm, has a large reddish purple disc with 8-13 short, blunt, orange arms, and is covered with regularly arranged spines. Found on coarse sand and gravel at extreme low water, and a predator of other starfish and bivalves, it is commoner than the larger **purple sunstar** *Solaster endeca* **4**. This has less obvious spines, is usually purple but may be orangey, and is absent from the south and south-east.

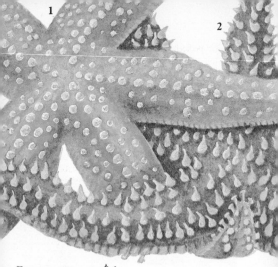

ECHINODERMS **starfish**

The commonest British shore starfish, which can be found in huge numbers where there are mussel beds, is the **common starfish** *Asterias rubens* **1**. It is a carnivore, feeding mainly on scallops and mussels, which it prizes open using its sucker tubefeet. It has 5 chubby, tapering arms and grows to 12 cm on shore, though offshore it may reach 45 cm. Brownish-apricot, it has many white knobs (spines), including a line down each arm. The **spiny starfish** *Marthasterias glacialis* **2** is larger, with fewer but very conspicuous pale spines, and a brownish or greenish, soft body. Both have minute

174

pincer-like pedicellariae among the spines (see pp. 168-9). The spiny starfish is not uncommon in the south and west at low water and below, where it feeds on scallops.

The **scarlet starfish** *Henricia oculata* **3**, 20 cm across, whose stiff, rounded, slender arms and relatively small disc are dark red or purple, is occasional on soft substrates. It is mainly sublittoral, as is the burrowing starfish *Astropecten irregularis* **4**, which can, however, also be found in sand at ELWS. Its flattened, orange or mauve body, 12-20 cm, has distinct limy plates, with spines all along the arms. The pointed tubefeet, well covered in mucus, allow it to sink vertically into the sand. It swallows bivalves, worms and crabs, ejecting the hard parts after digestion.

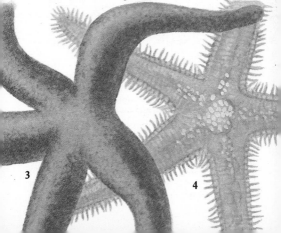

3

4

ECHINODERMS **brittlestars**

Brittlestars are very fragile and parts break off easily, but regenerate well. The species have characteristic arrangements of plates on the disc, but are still hard to identify. The **common brittlestar** *Ophiothrix fragilis* **1** is abundant low on all rocky shores, and turning a stone may reveal several writhing. The pentagonal disc (2 cm) can be bright purple, rusty or grey, with 5 rays of spines and, at the base of each arm, paired triangular plates which do not quite touch. Arms (10 cm) are pale-banded with long spines. Also common, especially among *Corallina* and where there is some sand and gravel, is the small, grey, sometimes phosphorescent *Amphipholis squamata* **2**, which is viviparous. The disc (5 mm) has a pale pair of contiguous plates at the base of each arm (2 cm). *Ophiocomina nigra* **3** occurs in the south and west among *Laminaria*, although it is really sublittoral. The disc (2.5 cm) is usually black but may be buff and finely granulated with no arm-base plates; the arms (12.5 cm) have clear bristly spines. The next two brittlestars burrow shallowly in sand. The **sandstar** *Ophiura texturata* **4** is mainly sublittoral, but leaves a birdsfoot-like mark on sand at low water, where it forages when covered. The orange disc (2.5 cm) has 4 plates, the outer pair with a comb edge, and 5 large white plates on the lower side. Arms (12.5 cm) arise from the top of the disc and have small spines pointing towards the tip. *Acrocnida brachiata* **5** has extremely long arms (18 cm) and a small grey disc (1.2 cm); in the south and west, low on shore.

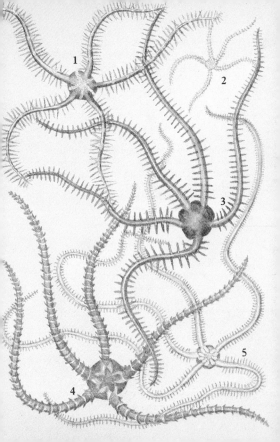

ECHINODERMS **sea urchins**

Sea urchins or echinoids have moveable spines and 5 pairs of rows of tubefeet. The beautiful limy test or skeleton may often be found, showing tubercles where the spines articulated and the pores through which the tubefeet protruded. The regular urchins here are spherical with strong spines, and are found low on rocky shores. The largest is the **edible** or **common sea urchin** *Echinus esculentus* **1**, 10 cm or more in diameter. It is sublittoral but can be found at low water especially in spring. Reddish, with red or white, solid, purple-tipped spines (1.5 cm), the test is pinkish when empty and has white tubercles. Its roes can be eaten.

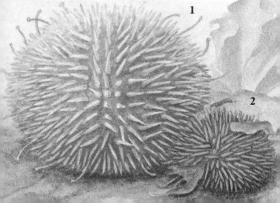

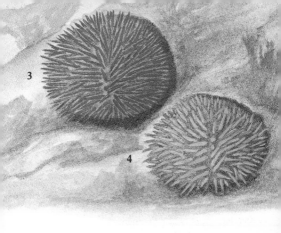

The **green sea urchin** *Psammechinus miliaris* **2**, up to 4 cm diameter, is green and its spines (1.5 cm) have purplish-brown tips, often adorned with pieces of weed. It is found under stones and in crevices low on rocky shores. The similar **rock urchin** *Paracentrotus lividus* **3** is confined to south and west Ireland and the Channel Is, but its long pointed spines (3 cm) are all dark purple, the test is flattened, and it lives, often gregariously, in hollows worn in rock by twisting spines and teeth. Also sometimes a rock borer, but only on the east coast is *Strongylocentrotus droebachiensis* **4**. Its green test has solid, blunt, ribbed spines, 2 cm, green, red or violet with pale tips.

179

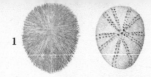

ECHINODERMS **cake and heart urchins**

The irregular urchins here have lost their primitive spherical shape and radial symmetry; their bilateral symmetry is a modification which aids burrowing. Cake urchins are oval and flattened and include the tiny **pea urchin** *Echinocyamus pusillus* **1**, to 1.5 cm, which may be found in or on gravelly sand at ELWS, though mainly sublittoral. Bright green or greyish, with many very short spines, it has 5 dorsal 'petals' of respiratory tube feet, and a ventral anus. The cast-up test is white.

The burrowing heart urchins below are not flattened, but heart-shaped with soft, backwards-pointing spines. They lack teeth, but collect debris from the sand surface with long, sticky, suckerless tube feet. Food is passed by the spines to the mouth, which is at the front of the animal—the anus is at the back. The anterior of the 5 dorsal petals extends as a groove to the mouth. Special broad spines underneath aid burrowing. The **purple heart urchin** *Spatangus purpureus* **2**, 12 cm long, has a greyish-mauve test in life. It occurs at ELWS and below in coarse sand and mud. The **sea potato** *Echinocardium cordatum* **3**, to 9 cm long, is however much commoner and burrows to 10 cm in clean sand on the lower part of the shore, a small hole showing on the surface. Its spines are sand-coloured and the fragile-yellowish tests are cast up.

ECHINODERMS **holothuroids**

All holothuroids are inactive, leathery-skinned and worm-like. 1-3 below occur uncommonly around low tide and below in crevices, under stones or on soft substrates in sheltered gullies mainly in the south-west.

The **cotton spinner** *Holothuria forskali* **1**, to 20 cm, has a clammy, thick, black warty skin above, and yellowish below with 3 rows of suckered tube-feet. Two furrows above mark the line of the reduced dorsal tubefeet. The mouth is surrounded by 20 short, retractile, yellow, feathery tubefeet, and when disturbed it ejects sticky white threads from the anus. The **sea gherkin** *Pawsonia saxicola* **2**, 15 cm, has 5 distinct rows of tubefeet, marked by brownish dots on its thin, smooth white skin. The 2 dorsal rows are single and zigzag; 10 long branched tubefeet surround the mouth and collect food into a mucous ball and pass it to the mouth.

The **sea cucumber** *Ocnus lacteus* **3** is smaller (4 cm), with few tubefeet in each row, a thicker, off-white or pinkish skin, and is more widely distributed, except in parts of the east. The burrowing **worm cucumber** *Leptosynapta inhaerens* **4**, 18 cm, occurs locally in sand and mud among *Zostera*, except in the north. Its transparent skin lacks tube-feet, but contains spicules which lend it an adhesive roughness, like Velcro, with which it gains purchase for movement. There are 12 branched tubefeet round the mouth.

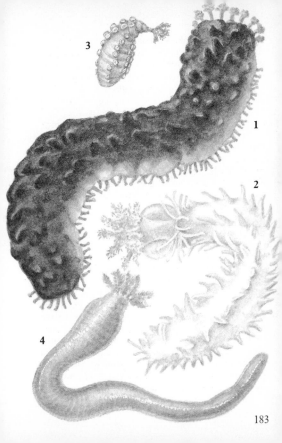

183

CHORDATES **sea squirts**

Sea squirts or ascidians are very common attached to weed, stones, rocks or man-made objects low on the shore. Water squirts out of the two siphons when squeezed, and the relative position of the siphons is important in identification. The soft, cylindrical, contractile *Ciona intestinalis* **1**, to 12 cm, is attached by its base to rock. The body contents are visible through the pale greenish-grey, semi-transparent tunic, which has 5 muscle bands in the wall and yellow edges to the tubular, orange-spotted siphons, placed close together near the top; common throughout. *Ascidiella aspersa* **2**, 6 cm, is estuarine and occurs in the south-west, often on piles and stones in mud. Similar in shape and often found in clusters, its knobbly, tough, brownish-grey tunic has the exhalant siphon ⅓ of the way down. *A. scabra* **3**, 1.5-5 cm, has a transparent, stiff, oval tunic, attached along most of one side. Its siphons are prominent, one at the end, the other about ¼ of the body length away; especially in the north. The thin, clear sac of *Ascidia conchilega* **4** is also attached along one side, but the exhalant siphon is further from the inhalant. Its tunic is slightly rough and body contents are visible through it; widespread. Common under overhangs, on stones, or on *Laminaria* stalks on exposed coasts, particularly in the south and west, is the **sea gooseberry** *Dendrodoa grossularia* **5**, to 1.2 cm across, whose squat, rusty-red tunic, wrinkled and tough, has well-separated scarlet siphons on the upper surface. Gregarious and sometimes fused at the base.

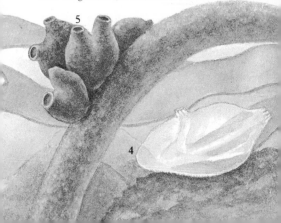

CHORDATES **sea squirts**

The sea squirts here are colonial, consisting either of groups of independent individuals or, in the compound ascidians, of more integrated groups. *Clavelina lepadiformis* **1** has a system of stolons from which soft, upright, vase-shaped individuals arise, up to 3 cm long, with siphons close together on top. The tunic is so transparent that the orangey body contents are visible; it is common around extreme low water on both solid structures and weed.

The next two species are compound ascidians, in which the individual zooids, although they have independent inhalant siphons, share a common exhalant siphon. The **star ascidian** *Botryllus schlosseri* **2** has zooids 2 mm long, embedded in a gelatinous test in groups of 3-12, forming stars around an exhalant opening. The colour is variable but can be violet with cream stars and a red spot on each zooid or lime-green with yellow stars. The patches, to 15 cm, encrust stones and weed from midshore down and are very common, especially in August. In sheltered positions it hangs down from overhangs. This sea squirt is very beautiful and worth observing through a lens.

Botrylloides leachi **3** has smaller zooids (1.5 mm) which are arranged in irregular branched lines or ovals, with long common openings. Orange, red or grey, it is found low on shore on stones and often on other sea squirts.

Fish: eels and pipefish

These fish are elongated and lack pelvic fins; eels have a continuous dorsal, tail and anal fin. In the **common eel** *Anguilla anguilla* **1** it starts well behind the gills, the pectoral fin is rounded and the lower jaw protrudes; in the **conger** *Conger conger* **2** the dorsal fin arises above the tip of the pectorals, which are pointed, and the upper jaw protrudes. Common eels (♀ 1 m, ♂ 50 cm) spawn in the Atlantic and shiny 3-year old elvers (7 cm) are common in estuaries in spring, as they return to the rivers, where they live as yellow eels. In autumn, some old and now silver eels return to the spawning grounds. The conger (to 2 m) is totally marine; strong and dark and common amongst weed at the edge of the sea, especially in the west; spawns in the Atlantic.

The **worm pipefish** *Nerophis lumbriciformis* **3**, 15 cm, is dark olive with white throat markings, and is rather rigid and worm-like. It has tiny dorsal fins only, and it sucks up its prey through its short, narrow snout. Well camouflaged among weed on all rocky coasts, in the west. In summer, the ♂ carries eggs in a belly pouch. The **lesser sand-eel** *Ammodytes tobianus* **4**, 15 cm, a narrow, silvery fish with protruding lower jaw, long single dorsal fin, anal fin and separate tail fin, occurs abundantly in summer, swimming in shoals at the water's edge or buried in clean sand, where it may be taken in shrimp nets. Sand-eels are a major part of the diet of puffins and many fish.

1 ♀ ♂

2

3

4

189

Fishes: **sticklebacks and gobies**

Two sticklebacks occur on the shore; both have pelvic fins reduced to spines and are olive above, silvery below. The ♂ builds and guards a nest of weeds about 10 cm across, in spring. The **15-spined stickleback** *Spinachia spinachia* 1, 15 cm, is common in rocky pools; as well as its 15 dorsal spines, its shape and fan-shaped tail fin are distinctive. In spring the ♀ is distended with eggs and the ♂ becomes darker. *Gasterosteus aculeatus* 2, the smaller (10 cm) and mainly freshwater **3-spined stickleback**, frequently occurs in brackish water. Its deeper body has dark dorsal markings, a shorter tail, and the ♂ has a red belly in spring.

Gobies are very common goggle-eyed fish, with pelvic fins modified into a sucker, a rounded tail fin, and 2 dorsal fins, the front usually with 6 flexible spines. Most are bottom-living, gregarious and well-camouflaged; ♂ guards eggs fiercely. The **common** or **sand goby** *Pomatoschistus microps* 3, 8 cm, lives on sand or mud in pools, or even high up estuaries and saltmarshes. Its greyish-brown body has 4 dusky saddles and a black spot on the front dorsal fin. The **2-spotted goby** *Gobiusculus flavescens* 4, 6 cm, has 7 spines on the front dorsal fin, and 2 dark spots on its mottled, yellow-brown body. It hovers among *Laminaria* and lays its eggs on the holdfasts. The sturdier, darkish brown body of the **rock goby** *Gobius paganellus* 5, 10 cm, has 4 equal front rays on the first dorsal fin, which is edged with pale orange, and free spines on the upper edge of the pectoral fins. Occurs singly among weed in pools, mainly in the south and west.

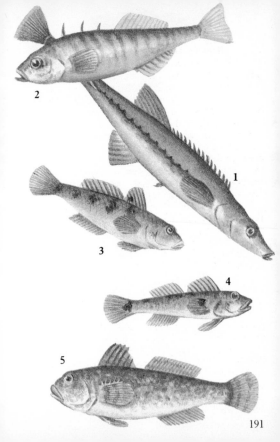

1

Fish: **sucker fish**

All these fish occur in pools low on rocky shores, are
bottom living, and can attach themselves firmly to
rocks by circular suckers on their belly, modified from
pelvic fins. The **lumpsucker** *Cyclopterus lumpus* **1**, to 55
cm, may be stranded at ELW in spring, mainly in the
north, as it comes inshore to spawn among weed. ♂'s
guard the eggs, which are eaten as imitation caviar.
Young, green lumpsuckers are often found in summer.
Adults have bulky, bulbous bodies with 4 rows of
tubercles on each side and no scales; the front dorsal
fin becomes thick and lumpy. Normally dark petrol-
blue, paler below, but breeding ♂'s become reddish.
The next two sucker fish lack tubercles and have a large
sucker ⅓ body length. They also migrate offshore in

winter. Commonest in the south and west is the **Cornish sucker** *Lepadogaster lepadogaster* **2**, 7 cm. Flattened below, with a pointed snout and reddish skin, it has 2 yellow-ringed black eyespots behind the eyes. Its tail fin is continuous with the dorsal and anal fins. Eggs in crevices, guarded by the ♂. Only the young of the smaller **2-spotted sucker** *Diplecogaster bimaculata* **3**, to 5 cm, are found on the shore. Orange, with red, V-shaped marks behind the eye, it has black spots behind the pectorals and a separate tail fin; all coasts. **Montagu's seasnail** *Liparis montagui* **4**, 8 cm, is frequent under rocks, among weed, and in estuaries. Its smooth, spotted, purplish-brown body has yellow, flecked fins, a blunt head, loose skin, a single long dorsal and shorter anal fin, and the pectorals meet beneath.

193

Fishes: **bullhead, wrasses and weever**

The mottled dark grey and yellow fins of the **bullhead** or **father-lasher** *Myoxocephalus scorpius* **1**, 12-20 cm, camouflage this inactive bottom dweller. Its gill covers, which it raises to threaten predators, have 4 spines, and there are 2 large yellow spiny dorsal fins. The ♂ fiercely guards the yellow eggs, laid in shells. The **long-spined sea scorpion** *Taurulus bubalis* **2** is smaller and more colourful, and has 5 gill-cover spines, one longer than the rest. Both occur on all rocky coasts, particularly in the north and in summer. The two wrasses here come ashore to breed, making loose nests of weed; the young are greenish. Wrasses have deep, narrow bodies, a single spiny dorsal fin, thick lips, strong teeth and colourful mottled scales, and feed on crustacea, including barnacles, and worms. The **ballan wrasse** *Labrus bergylta* **3**, 25-60 cm, has a humped forehead, spines on the front ⅔ of the dorsal fin, and pale-centred scales. The smaller **corkwing** *Crenilabrus melops* **4**, 10-25 cm, with a toothed front gill cover, is variable, often spotted rust and green. It has dark bands across the head and a dark spot where the lateral line joins the tail. Common in pools in the south. The **lesser weever** or **stingfish** *Echiichthys vipera* **5**, 12 cm, lives buried in sand, except for its eyes and slanting mouth. Pelvic fins are in front of the pectorals. It stuns shrimps by raising the black front dorsal fin and injecting poison along the 5 grooved spines and the gill-cover spines; if touched, the venom causes extreme pain and swelling, like a severe bee-sting, which subsides after some hours; commonest in the south-west.

Fish: **flatfish**

Young flatfish can be found half-buried in sandy pools or muddy bays. Initially, as planktonic larvae, they have a normal fish shape, but after a couple of months one eye moves to the other side and the fish becomes bottom-living; the dorsal and ventral fins extend and the underside pales. Flatfish can alter their depth of colour to blend, and cover themselves with sand by undulating the single fins. The fish on this plate have their right sides uppermost.

Plaice *Pleuronectes platessa* **1**, to 40 cm, are very common, especially in the N. Sea, but young fish (8-12 cm) are often found on sandy shores and in estuary mouths, where they feed on worms, shrimps and bivalves by day. Greenish-brown with orange spots above and greyish below, they have a straight lateral line and a line of about 4 knobs between the eyes. The **flounder** *Platichthys flesus* **2** is similar, but has less distinct spots, knobs where the single fins join the body and along the lateral line, and the dorsal fin starts near the eye. They are very tolerant of low salinity and are found high up estuaries, especially in summer. They occur on all coasts and breed at sea in winter. The **dab** *Limanda limanda* **3** is smaller, and lacks the knobs, but has rough scales. It is brown with only vague markings, grey beneath, and with a curved lateral line. It lives on sandy bottoms and estuary mouths, and is common in late summer.

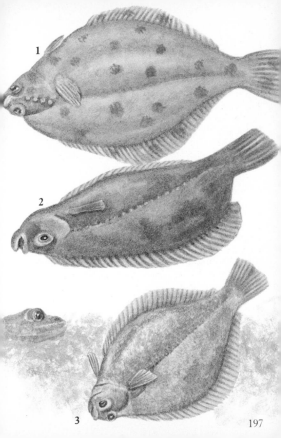

197

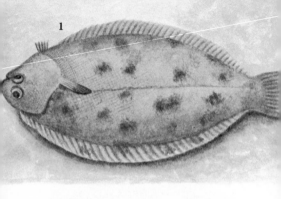

1

Fish: **flatfish**

The **sole** *Solea solea* **1** comes in to shallow water to spawn in summer and specimens up to 40 cm (though more often nearer 12 cm) may be found in sandy or muddy bays, particularly in the south. Like the plaice (p. 196), the sole lies right side upwards, but it hunts at night, locating prey with the sensitive hairs on the lower side of its blunt head. Its mouth is not at the end of the body, but towards the pelvic fin, which is only just separated from the long anal fin. The mid-brown, oval body has indistinct blotches, with a black patch on the pectoral fin, and is white beneath.

Both the **turbot** *Scophthalmus maximus* **2** and the **brill** *S. rhombus* **3** lie left side uppermost. Turbot may grow to over 60 cm, on coarse, gravelly sand, where they feed on other fish, with their large mouth and teeth. The body is round in outline, the upper surface scaleless, warty, and brown-speckled, and the lower white. The dorsal fin starts between the mouth and the eyes, and the tail fin is spotted. Turbot are a delicacy. Young fish (5-8 cm) can be caught at the water line, especially in the south, in summer. The brill is very similar but smaller, with scales but no warts, a greenish skin with dark blotches, and no tail spots.

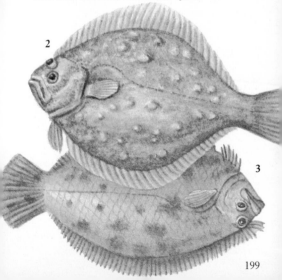

Fish: **blennies and butterfish**

There are many species of blenny, all of which have large eyes, a single dorsal fin, and pelvic fins in front of the large round pectorals. They are found in weedy pools, often with sandy bottoms, or under stones uncovered by the tide. The commonest all year round is the **active shanny** or **common blenny** *Lipophrys pholis* **1**, whose thickset, dark green or khaki body, to 12 cm but often less, has thick lips, black mottling, and a continuous dorsal fin, notched in the middle. The anal fin is half the length of the dorsal fin, and the pelvics consist of 2 rays which help support the fish on the bottom or as it 'crawls' on the rocks. Its strong teeth rasp barnacles and mussels off rocks and can bite a finger. The golden eggs are laid in crevices in early summer, and are guarded by the then almost black male.

The **butterfish** *Pholis gunnellus* **2**, so called because of its very slippery skin, is also abundant all year. The long, laterally flattened, rather eel-like body, to 15 cm, is golden-grey, with 10-13

distinct, white-encircled black spots along the base of the long, spiny dorsal fin. The tail fin is rounded. In winter the ♀ lays a yellow egg mass, 3 cm (sometimes in shells) which both parents may curl round to guard. The **viviparous blenny** or **eelpout** *Zoarces viviparus* **3** is larger, to 40 cm, with no tail fin, and a notch near the tail in the dorsal fin, which is continuous with the anal fin. As its name implies this blenny is viviparous, and mating occurs in late summer. The early development of the embryo takes place inside the mother and the ♀ lays about 200 live young in winter, which is spent offshore. Viviparity means that fewer young are produced, but the dangerous egg stage is avoided, and more of them survive. It is common in the north and east, especially in summer, among rocks and also in the brackish water of estuaries.

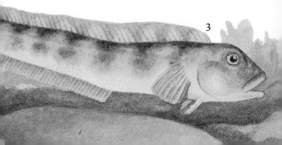

Fish: **rocklings and gurnard**

Rocklings have slim bodies with their pelvic fins in front of the pectoral fins, and with a long anal and a rounded tail fin. The 2 dorsal fins run along most of the back, but the front one, except for a pronounced first ray, is sunk in a groove, and has a sensory function. The **5-bearded rockling** Ciliata mustela **1**, 15-30 cm, is blackish-green, shading to paler below, with dark fins and 5 sensory barbels— 1 on the chin, 2 on the upper lip, and 1 from each nostril; it is common near the bottom of intertidal pools, among weed, on all coasts, including estuaries. These and other rock-pool fish, such as blennies, are easy to catch with a net and baited line. The **3-bearded rockling** Gaidropsarus vulgaris **2**, 15-40 cm, is dull brown, with dark blotches when adult, paler below and with only 3 barbels. It lives mainly offshore, where it breeds, but it occurs under stones and weed on shore in the south and south-west.

Found in low pools and shallow water on all coasts, the **grey gurnard** Eutrigla gurnardus **3**, to 40 cm, is well adapted to bottom-living and feeding, with its mouth low on the head, and 3 sensory rays modified from each pectoral fin, used for 'crawling' over soft surfaces. It has an armoured head, pointed snout, spiny scales along the lateral line, and is grey with cream spots. The first dorsal fin is tall and spiny, and the second mirrors the anal fin. Unusually among fish, most of which are silent, it can grunt when disturbed.

Birds on cliffs

The birds on this plate are not seabirds, in the sense that they never get themselves wet, but they are so characteristic of sea-cliffs that any seashore visitor especially in the west is sure to see them. Two crows commonly nest on cliffs, but they cannot be confused. The **raven** *Corvus corax* **1** is much the largest wholly black bird in Britain, and in flight is given away by its massive bill, wedge-shaped tail, and deep, croaking call; often rolls and tumbles in flight. Ravens start nesting as early as February, building a stout pile of twigs on a cliff ledge; mainly in Cornwall, Wales and Scotland. The much smaller **jackdaw** *Corvus monedula* **2** is found on all coasts and prefers to nest in holes, and flies in flocks, calling loudly various staccato notes. The larger hooded crow *Corvus corone cornix*, restricted to Scotland and Ireland, is also black and grey, but has black wings and head, whereas the jackdaw's grey is on the back of its head. True **rock doves** *Columba livia* **3** are now found almost exclusively in Scotland and Ireland, and any coastal dove seen elsewhere will probably be a feral pigeon, the pigeon of towns and parks, which is itself descended from the rock dove. Interbreeding between feral pigeons and the wild rock doves occurs. It nests on cliffs, often in sea-caves, but feeds in inland fields. **Rock pipits** *Anthus spinoletta* **4** can be seen on rocky coasts all around Britain, and it is the only small brown bird which habitually feeds among rocks by the shore. In the breeding season it indulges in an almost lark-like song-flight, gathering momentum and ending in a long trill as it glides back to earth.

Birds: **terns**

Terns are among the most graceful of birds, skimming along with lazy wing-beats above the water and suddenly folding their narrow, pointed wings to dive for a fish. All have rather harsh calls, white bodies with grey wings and a black cap; they nest in colonies, often of more than one species, and fiercely attack intruders.

Common tern *Sterna hirundo* **1** and **arctic tern** *S. paradisaea* **2** are extremely hard to distinguish in the field. Common tern has longer legs when standing, and a more orangey-red bill with a black tip. Both occur all around the coast, though the arctic tern becomes commoner further north, and they breed on shingle-banks and sand-dunes, sometimes together. Both are summer visitors, but whereas the common tern winters off Africa, the arctic tern may travel as far as Antarctica.

Little tern *S. albifrons* **3** is much the smallest tern, about the size of a blackbird. Unlike the common tern, both legs and bill are yellow, and its black cap has a conspicuous white forehead. It is rather rare, breeding in small colonies, few and far between; another summer visitor, it too winters in the tropics.

The **Sandwich tern** *S. sandvicensis* **4** is the largest species to breed in Britain, and noticeably heavier in flight. It has very pale grey wings, black legs, a yellow-tipped black bill, and its black cap is often raised at the back of the head into a short crest. Though it has few breeding colonies, they tend to be large, and they are scattered discontinuously round the British Isles. In winter British birds can be found along much of the coast of Africa.

207

Birds: **small gulls and fulmar**

Gulls are perhaps the quintessential seabirds, though many are common enough inland. They have white bodies, long grey or black wings, sometimes a black head, and usually pink or yellow legs. They breed in colonies, but unlike terns (pp. 206-7) are resident. Confusingly they often change plumage in winter, and young birds may have brownish plumage for the first year or two. The **black-headed gull** *Larus ridibundus* 1 and the **little gull** *L. minutus* 2 both have dark heads. The little gull is much smaller, has the hood extending down the back of its neck; it does not breed in Britain and is most often seen on the south and east coasts. Black-headed gulls are very common, on coasts and inland, breeding often on marshes and lake islands, as well as sand dunes. Both have rather tern-like flight and both lose their dark hoods in winter—all bar a tiny spot behind the eye—when the smaller size and dark underwing of the little gull are still distinctive.

Kittiwakes *Rissa tridactyla* **3** are cliff-breeding gulls, often in huge colonies. They get their name from their distinctive cry and are best told from the similar **common gull** *Larus canus* **4**, by their pure black wingtips—in the common gull this is interrupted by white spots. However the common gull is far from being the commonest breeding gull. The **fulmar** *Fulmarus glacialis* **5** is another cliff-breeder, but it is a petrel not a gull, distinguished by the conspicuous tube nostrils on the top of its bill. It has a most graceful gliding flight, with wings held stiff. Never approach a breeding fulmar—it will cover you with evil-smelling oil.

Birds: **large gulls**

These three gulls, and particularly the great black-back, are noticeably larger than any of the others. The **herring gull** *Larus argentatus* **1** is the commonest of the three and resembles a large common gull (p. 208), but can be distinguished by its pink, not greenish-yellow legs, as well as its size. The wings can vary from very pale to quite dark grey, when it becomes hard to separate from the **lesser black-backed gull** *L. fuscus* **2**. Again the legs are important, the lesser black-back's being yellow. The herring gull is found right round the northern hemisphere, whereas the lesser black-back is confined to Europe. The **greater black-backed gull** *L. marinus* **3** is noticeably larger and has very black wings; the lesser may have black wings, too, but the great black-back, like the herring gull, has flesh-coloured legs. All three breed singly or in colonies, on cliff ledges or, particularly the lesser black-back, on the ground. All three, too, have a conspicuous red spot on their yellow bills, which the chicks peck at to make the adults disgorge food.

Immature birds have less well-defined plumage, brown at first and then greyish, and not reaching the adult state until their third summer. An immature herring gull is shown **4**, but is virtually identical to immature lesser black-back.

Birds: auks

Auks are rather squat, black and white seabirds which nest on cliffs or in burrows but spend all the rest of their time at sea. They often sit on the water in huge rafts and are very vulnerable to oil pollution. They dive readily and in flight have very fast wing-beats.

Razorbill *Alca torda* **1** and **guillemot** *Uria aalge* **2** are the two largest species, since the extinction of the great auk. The razorbill has a strange flattened, white-barred bill, from which comes its name, and which distinguishes it from the otherwise similar guillemot, which is however brown rather than black. Both nest colonially on cliff ledges, laying a single egg, pear-shaped so that it does not roll off. When swimming they have a rather duck-like appearance. The **black guillemot** *Cepphus grylle* **3** resembles a small guillemot, but is entirely black, except for a prominent white patch on its wing, and it has conspicuous red legs and feet. In winter it is mostly white, with black and white barred wings. It breeds in small, rather scattered groups, usually in crevices near the base of cliffs, and mainly in Scotland and Ireland. An adult **puffin** *Fratercula arctica* **4** is quite impossible to confuse with any other seabird, with its huge and colourful bill. Young birds have much thinner bills, but can still be told by the white face. Puffins are very colonial nesters, often in great numbers, in burrows on cliff-tops, scattered along most rocky coasts, and preferably on islands for freedom from predators. The parents encourage the young to leave the nest by abandoning them after about 6 weeks, letting hunger do the rest.

Birds: **cormorants, gannet and heron**

The **shag** *Phalacrocorax aristotelis* **1** and the **cormorant** *P. carbo* **2** are closely related. The shag's plumage is uniformly a beautiful iridescent greenish-black, but the rather larger cormorant is browning on its back and has white patches on its throat and, in the breeding season, on its thighs as well. They often sit with their wings spread, drying; they swim low in water, head tilted upwards and bill raised, before diving. In flight they hold their long necks straight.

The shag is a more northern species and is restricted to rocky coasts, whereas the cormorant frequents estuaries and muddy shores too, feeding mainly on flatfish.

The **gannet** *Sula bassana* **3** is one of the most handsome and distinctive sea birds, and is the only British member of the booby family. In flight it is easily recognised by its long straight wings, with conspicuous pointed black tips; it catches fish by folding its wings and diving into the sea, often from a considerable height. Gannnets breed in densely packed colonies, often of huge size, and almost always on islands—there are famous colonies on the Bass Rock and Ailsa Craig; the only mainland nests are at Bempton in Yorkshire.

Although **herons** *Ardea cinerea* **4** are mainly fresh-water birds, they can often be seen feeding in quiet bays and estuaries, particularly in west Scotland where there is a paucity of suitable freshwater to feed on.

3

Birds: sea ducks and geese

Many ducks are found in coastal waters in winter, but rather few breed there in summer. The **eider** *Somateria mollissima* **1** is the most marine of British ducks, nesting in colonies on the ground in grassy or rocky places by the sea. Its nest is lined with feathers, collected commercially in places and used for filling eiderdowns. The ♂ is quite unmistakeable, but the ♀ is a dull barred brown, like so many female ducks, and is best identified by the characteristic sloping bill. **Shelducks** *Tadorna tadorna* **2** also nest by the sea, in burrows, often among sand dunes. Male and female are very similar, with chestnut breast-band and green head, but the ♂ has a conspicuous knob, like a mute swan's, above its bill. In winter shelducks often collect in estuaries. The **common scoter** *Melanitta nigra* **3** only breeds in Britain in the north of Scotland and north-west Ireland, but it can be seen off the coast anywhere in winter. It is a large duck, and the ♂ is all a greeny-black, unlike any other species. The ♀ is brownish, but can be recognised by its pale lower face. Many geese come to Britain in the winter from the high arctic, and most congregate in estuaries and on salt-flats, feeding on nearby fields. Only one species is trictly maritime, resting actually on the water and feeding on eel-grasses *Zostera* at low tide, and that is the **brent goose** *Branta bernicla*. It is a small, duck-sized goose, and unlike the larger and now widespread Canada goose has a wholly black head. The dark-breasted race *B. b. bernicla* shown here **4** breeds in arctic Russia and occurs mainly in eastern Britain, whereas the light-breasted form *B. b. hrota*, which winters mainly in western Britain, breeds in Greenland and Spitzbergen.

1 ♂ ♀

2

3

4

Birds: **divers**

Divers are large diving birds that breed from the Arctic south to Scotland, usually on small islands on lakes in moorland areas. They often fish at sea, close into shore, and spend all the non-breeding season at sea as well. They dive from a swimming position, like cormorants, but can be told from them by the way in which they hold the bill while swimming—level in divers, tilted up in cormorants.

The largest of the divers is the **great northern diver** *Gavia immer* **1**, shown here in winter plumage, as it is an arctic species, whose closest breeding haunts are in Iceland; it winters in British waters from September to May, particularly in the north. It is in fact more often seen than the smaller **black-throated diver** *Gavia arctica* **2**, though that breeds sparsely in north-west Scotland. The black-throated has a more slender bill, more sloping forehead and white thigh patches, and in winter, when it resembles the great northern more closely, its grey (rather than black) crown and neck are also good diagnostic features. The **red-throated diver** *Gavia stellata* **3** (summer) and **4** (winter) is much the commonest diver, and smaller still. In summer its striped neck and red throat patch are characteristic, but at all seasons it can be identified by its curiously upward-angled bill. In summer, when they are breeding on tiny inland lochans, red-throated divers are often seen flying between the nest and the feeding ground at sea, and their eerie wailing cry is heard.

Birds: skuas, Manx shearwater and storm petrel

Skuas are the bird pirates of the seashore, obtaining their food by pursuing other birds, particularly gulls, until they disgorge their catch. They also defend their nests fiercely against all intruders, and will readily attack a man. A blow from a **'bonxie'** or **great skua** *Stercorarius skua* **1** will not be easily forgotten, for it is a large bird, the size of an immature herring gull, which it rather resembles. It can be distinguished by its heavier build, the white wing patches, and above all by its behaviour. Great skuas breed on moorland, mostly in Orkney and Shetland, but winter in the N. Atlantic and are sometimes seen off other coasts in passage. **Arctic skuas** *Stercorarius parasiticus* **2** are smaller and more numerous, and have two prominently projecting feathers from the middle of the tail. They may have either the creamy-

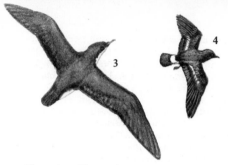

white neck and breast shown (pale phase), or else be all sooty brown (dark phase); confusing intermediate plumage types are sometimes seen too. They breed in N. Scotland, and winter in the S. Atlantic, and are often seen on passage.

Shearwaters get their name from their flight, gliding stiff-winged and angled so that one wing tip seems to 'shear' the water; they are related to albatrosses. The **Manx shearwater** *Puffinus puffinus* **3** breeds on a few islands off the West coast, Shetland and Orkney, in burrows and often in very large numbers. It comes ashore only to breed, only therefore in summer and only at night, so is most likely to be seen at sea, sometimes sitting on the water in huge 'rafts'. The **storm petrel** *Hydrobates pelagicus* **4** is another nocturnal breeder with a similar distribution, and is most often seen from ships, when it can be seen flying low with feet dangling, apparently walking on the water. It is the smallest seabird, and all black except for its white rump and wingbars.

Birds: **waders**

Waders are long-legged and mostly long-billed shore birds that feed on sandy and muddy shores, probing for worms, crabs and snails, or else chasing the receding waves and picking up creatures uncovered by them. Some can be hard to identify, and a specialist bird book is needed for the smaller brown ones. But the **oystercatcher** *Haematopus ostralegus* **1** is instantly recognisable, by its combination of black and white plumage, orange bill and pink legs, and by its penetrating piping call. It breeds all round the coast and the eggs are laid on the ground, on sand, shingle or among rocks. The **curlew** *Numenius arquata* **2** is another large wader with a familiar call—sounding just like its name. It breeds on moors, but out of the breeding season is common in muddy estuaries, where it probes with its long, down-turned bill—the much rarer black and white avocet has an upturned bill with which it sweeps in shallow water.

The **redshank** *Tringa totanus* **3** is also mainly a moorland breeder, though non-breeding birds and some breeding pairs can be found on the coast in summer as well as winter. It is a grey-brown bird, with conspicuous red legs and a penetrating call; in flight it is easily recognised by the white trailing edge to the wing. It is common throughout the year, whereas the **knot** *Calidris canuta* **4** is a winter visitor, which breeds in the high Arctic. It is a very grey bird and often occurs in huge flocks.

Birds: **small waders**

The **dunlin** *Calidris alpina* **1** (summer) and **2** (winter) is the commonest small wader and, like many others, breeds on moorlands and mountains, though non-breeding individuals can be seen by the sea all summer. Then they can easily be recognised by the black breast-patch, but in winter they look like many other waders—look for the slightly down-curved bill. They flock in large numbers, and groups fly with astonishing precision, wheeling and turning as one. The slightly larger **sanderling** *Calidris alba* **3** is another winter visitor, but it is much paler—almost white underneath. It frequents sandy shores and prefers to run than to fly; it feeds on sandhoppers and other small animals disturbed by the tide, and chases the waves, its legs moving so fast that it appears to be on rollers.

Another very common small shore bird is the **ringed plover** *Charadrius hiaticula* **4**, which is less sociable, however. The black and white-barred face, short stubby bill and orangey legs are quite distinctive, as is its behaviour. It runs rapidly about the shore, and bobs up and down nervously if approached. Its nest is simply a depression in sand or shingle, but the eggs are well camouflaged. Ringed plovers are birds of sandy and shingly shores, whereas the **turnstone** *Arenaria interpres* **5** lives on weed-covered rocky shores, and gets its name from its habit of turning over stones when looking for food. It is mainly a winter visitor, when its plumage is largely black and white, but non-breeding birds in the handsome summer plumage—chestnut-brown, black and white—also occur.

Mammals: **otter and seals**

Several mammals are casual visitors to the shore, and rats are common scavengers, particularly near ports, but none of these land mammals feed in the water. Of the marine mammals, whales and dolphins never come ashore, except when inexplicably stranded, and seals feed at sea and come ashore only to breed and to rest. Surprisingly, the mammal that uses the seashore habitat most is the **otter** *Lutra lutra* **1**. Otters are normally thought of as freshwater animals, but on rocky coasts in N and W Scotland, they are as common as anywhere in Britain. Some breed on the coast, in caves and holes in cliffs, and others move there when food is hard to find inland; they feed mainly on fish, crabs, and crustaceans. A full grown otter is from 1 to 1.3 m long, up to ⅓ of which may consist of the powerful tail, with which it swims. Otters travel equally well on land or in water, but seals are most ungainly on land, because their limbs have become modified into flippers and they are superb swimmers. Seals feed by diving for fish, crabs and various shellfish, and they typically remain submerged for 5-10 minutes, though dives of up to 45 have been recorded; they achieve this by metabolic adaptations which permit them to go without breathing for these long periods. **Common seals** *Phoca vitulina* **2** are 1.5 to 2 m long, rather yellowish grey and densely spotted. They occur in colonies on both rocky and sandy coasts, but particularly in estuaries, where they may be seen hauled out on sandbars. The common seal has a more dog-like face, with pronounced forehead and snout, than the larger **grey seal** *Halichoerus grypus* **3**, which has a patchy rather than a spotty grey coat. It frequents quiet, rocky shores, where the white pups may be found in autumn. An endangered species elsewhere, probably 70-80% of the world population are on British shores.

5   6

Mammals: **whales and dolphins**

Whales are of two types: baleen whales that live on plankton filtered from the water, are large, and rather rare in British waters; and toothed whales, which feed on fish. Dolphins and porpoises are toothed whales. The **common dolphin** *Delphinus delphis* **1** is the one most often seen following ships, most of which it can easily outpace. It frequently leaps clear of the water, when its pale flanks and curved, pointed dorsal fin can be seen. It reaches 2.6 m. The **bottle-nosed dolphin** *Tursiops truncatus* **2** is larger (to 3.5 m) and all grey, and less gracefully built. Both are playful and intelligent, and live typically in small schools. The **common porpoise** *Phocaena phocaena* **3** is always less than 2 m, with a rounded snout and a very small dorsal fin. This and the much larger **pilot whale** *Globicephala melaena* **4** are the two whales most·commonly stranded, as an as yet unexplained behaviour which can lead to the deaths of whole schools. Many other whales can be seen from time to time around British shores, but usually all that is visible is a fin. A very tall straight dorsal fin moving at speed is likely to be that of a **killer whale** *Orcinus orca* **5**, in which the male is twice the size of the female. Killer whales are in fact large but ferocious dolphins, feeding on seals and smaller dolphins. By contrast, a

large, slow-moving triangular fin, often in front of a narrower tail fin, belies the presence, not of a whale, but of the **basking shark** *Cetorhinus maximus* **6**, a fish, not a mammal. Indeed it is the second largest of all fish, but unlike some sharks quite harmless, for it feeds on plankton like baleen whales, and can sometimes be seen on migration off the west coast in autumn.

The strandline

Many interesting things can be found on the strandline, especially after storms. Delicate sublittoral reds are among the weeds cast up, as well as hornwrack *Flustra foliacea* **1**, whose beige frond, about 6 cm, resembles faded seaweed. It is in fact a seamat (pp. 170-1) and the frond is a honeycomb of tiny capsules. Typically the sandhopper *Talitrus saltator* (pp. 152-3) scavenges the strandline, and cast-up carapaces of the masked crab *Corystes* (pp. 162-3), shore crab *Carcinus* (pp. 160-1) and tests of sea-urchins are soon picked clean by gulls. Shells of cockles, razors and gapers can be numerous, and driftwood may well have superficial holes, 5 mm diameter, made by the gribble *Limnoria lignorum* (pp. 148-9), or lime-encrusted holes, perfectly round and 1.5 cm across, the work of the shipworm *Teredo* (pp. 124-5). A cuttlefish bone **2** of *Sepia officinalis* (pp. 138-9), white, oval and light, to 15 cm, is a good find, as are goose barnacles *Lepas* (pp. 144-5), attached to wood or a bottle. Jellyfish, such as *Aurelia* (pp. 76-7), are often left stranded, as are the light, round, beige clusters of empty egg cases of common whelk *Buccinum undatum* **3** (pp. 118-9). The lesser spotted dogfish *Scyliorhinus caniculus* attaches its egg case, the mermaid's purse **4** to weeds. After many months the young fish bursts out, and the empty cases, each with 4 tendrils, may come ashore. Those of skates do not have twisting tendrils. In regions where there are cliffs of Jurassic or Cretaceous rocks (190-65 million years old), ammonites **5** and belemnites **6** may be found on the shore.

230

Index of English Names

233

234

235

Index of Scientific Names

237

239